SAVED SINGLES SURVIVING

a Seductive Society

SAVED SINGLES SURVIVING

a Seductive Society

Dr. Allen S. Turner

Tate Publishing & *Enterprises*

Published by Tate Publishing & Enterprises, LLC
127 E. Trade Center Terrace | Mustang, Oklahoma 73064 USA
1.888.361.9473 | www.tatepublishing.com

Tate Publishing is committed to excellence in the publishing industry. The company reflects the philosophy established by the founders, based on Psalm 68:11,
"The Lord gave the word and great was the company of those who published it."

Interior design by Nathan Harmony

Published in the United States of America

ISBN: 978-1-60696-121-6
1. Nonfiction: Single Living
2. Spiritual Growth
08.10.06

Dedication

Although I have many people to thank for inspiring me, I want to dedicate this book to my Father in heaven. He is my protector, my provider, and my everything. Thank you, Father, for always being there for me and never leaving me.

I want to also dedicate this book to my dad, Dr. Allen Turner, who went home to be with Lord. Dad, I will see you again in glory.

This book also is dedicated to my mom, who is my biggest supporter and who always made sure I stayed rooted and grounded in the Lord.

To my wonderful wife and beautiful children, you all are the best. I love you all so much.

To my church family, you all know how much your pastor loves and appreciates you. SMBC for Life!

To Bishop Ernestine C. Reems-Dickerson, Mom, you have been a wonderful example on how to keep prayer the essential key to continued power in God.

To Bishop Bob Jackson, thank you for always being an example of how to walk upright before the Lord.

Acknowledgments

First of all, I would like to thank God the Father, God the Son, and God the Holy Ghost, who are all one, for this spiritual assignment and using me as a scribe to give your message to the world. To my angel and wife, Yolanda Roschelle Turner. Without her dedication, her consecration, her intercession, and her love for me, this project would not have been successful. Yolanda, you are truly a helpmate and a best friend. I love you and will always be your honey.

Table of Contents

Foreword

Welcome to Dr. Allen S. Turner's latest release, *Saved Singles Surviving a Seductive Society.* If you are single for whatever reason, this book is for you. You will discover godly principles on how to make it as a single man or woman and how to find out what God has in store for you. You will discover what blessings God has kept in store for you since the foundations of the earth and how to get them all.

In this life-changing book, single man or woman, get ready to step into the next dimension in God. You will never be the same after reading this book. I recommend this book to every single person in the world. *Saved Singles Surviving a Seductive Society* will truly go down in history as one of the best books for single Christians ever written.

Bishop Ernestine C. Reems-Dickerson
Senior Pastor, Center of Hope Church
Oakland, California

Introduction

Have you ever asked yourself why God has you single? Another question I asked God was why He allows being single to be so hard in such a seductive society. There are media, TV, and movies making you feel the emotional, sexual, and relational issues of life, peers, our families, our past and current relationships, and our own flesh battles to get us to go against God's Word. You have to deal with lack of companionship, sexual appetites, loneliness, struggling to afford to live on a single-household income in a dual income society, raising children as a single parent, trying to find out what God wants to be crucified in yourself before He gives me my companion, trying to learn how to praise God for the blessing that is not here yet, security and safety concerns while being single, having a desire to meet the right one with limited resources and places to meet them, and just missing that helping hand when no one is there. There is a special group of people in the church who battle these issues that are looked over, and they are widows. How do you go from having companionship, sex whenever you want it, arms holding you, safety and security, a shoulder to cry on, a friend to talk to, etc, to not having this at all but yet trying to suppress a hunger that is used to being fed?

In this book I want to show you biblical principles on how God sees you at this juncture or season of your life, and what His will for you individually is.

1 Lack of Companionship

One crucial need for any person, single or married, is the need for companionship. I just want someone who can just be there for me. Be my buddy, best friend, my shoulder to cry on, someone to share my dreams with, and someone just to hear me and give me the support I need.

One important message to any single man or woman is that many married folk don't have companionship. So remember that getting married does not ensure you get companionship. Some are married, but their loved one doesn't listen; married but they don't care for their mate; married but their mate doesn't support them; married but they aren't really loved for their true selves. So then the question is, should I settle for any man or woman and hope they fill this void, or do I learn the lesson of true companionship with my first love, Jesus Christ, so I can know what to look for in companionship.

This book will give lessons on mastering the fulfillment of your needs so you know what to look for in a mate and how to give to your new mate.

Webster defines *companionship* "as the relationship or connection between two people that associates them by similarities in character or desires as they accompany or keep company with each other as they aid and live with each other."[1]

Single brother or sister everyone needs companionship, and you deserve it. The question for you is, do you want to experience the real thing or do you want the mature one first, so you never have to hunger for it while you are enduring the immature version with that new companion. God is the type of God that always wants His children to experience the best, so they should look for the best. I have three daughters named Adojinah, Alaisha, and Ashley. One of my strongest convictions is to make sure that I give them the best so they always expect the best. I take them to the best restaurants, the best shopping malls and stores, on the best vacations, and give them a lot of attention because I want them to expect it to that extent from any man that comes into their lives. A brother better come correct or not come at all because I have given them the expectation. Man of God or woman of God, don't get mad at God for wanting to keep mediocrity or average from you so you can experience the best, which is from Him.

Let me show you some brothers and sisters who found true companionship in God. Read Genesis 29:30–35 where Moses writes of Jacob,

> And he went in also unto Rachel, and he loved also Rachel more than Leah, and served with [Laban] yet seven other years. 31. And when the Lord saw that Leah was hated, he opened her womb: but Rachel was barren. 32. And Leah conceived, and bare a son, and she called his name Reuben: for she said, Surely the Lord hath looked upon my affliction; now therefore

> my husband will love me. 33. And she conceived again, and bare a son; and said, Because the Lord hath heard that I was hated, he hath therefore given me this son also: and she called his name Simeon. 34. And she conceived again, and bare a son; and said, Now this time will my husband be joined unto me, because I have born him three sons: therefore was his name called Levi. 35. And she conceived again, and bare a son: and she said, Now will I praise the Lord: therefore she called his name Judah; and left bearing.

Leah had a man, but he loved Rachel more than her. You may get or have had a man or woman, but if that person had other interests such as: profession, another man or woman, sports, the other family, etc., then you know how Leah felt.

Marriage does not guarantee companionship. Leah may have thought that Jacob would give her true companionship. She did what we all have done to win love: she gave up her total self, expecting just a little in return. Look at what she said after she got pregnant, hoping to win his love. She said, "I bare him a son, now surely my man will love me" (Genesis 29:32). Guess what, he didn't!

The following verses explain that she tried two more times to win affection, but he still hated her and would not join himself to her.

My brother and sister, when God wants you to experience the best, He will make the imposters do things to put bitterness in your mouth. Finally after Leah saw only God could be her true companion, she said "Now will I praise [give honor, attention, and love] to the Lord" (Genesis 29:35).

In other words, there is someone who wants to be my true companion, and His name is Jesus Christ.

The need for companionship stems from the beginning of mankind when God made man and woman: "And the Lord God said, It is not good that the man should be alone; I will make an help meet for him" (Genesis 2:18). God in His omniscient (all knowing) character knew that man would not always walk hand in hand with God in true companionship. As we know, when Adam and Eve sinned in the Garden of Eden, this thereby confirmed that man no longer could walk with God. For when God came to the garden looking for Adam for their time together, Adam hid and was afraid to come into relationship with God because of his sin. Of the sin Adam and Eve committed, God said in Genesis 6:3 "And the Lord said, My spirit shall not always strive [rule] with man, for that he also is flesh." In other words I (God) cannot be a true companion with man; because sin dwells in him, we are incompatible. God we praise for Jesus Christ, because we are more than just flesh (or bodies) we are also spirit beings. The true need for you to survive is not your flesh, but your spirit. Your spirit man was dead in sin through Adam, but once you accepted Christ in your life the spirit was quickened or made alive; and now your relationship with God has been reconciled. God wanted companionship with you so badly that He was willing to give His son, Jesus Christ, as a sacrifice for your love. In 2 Corinthians 5:18–19, God was in Christ bringing you back to Him. The Apostle Paul writes,

> And all things are of God, who hath reconciled us to himself by Jesus Christ, and hath given to us

> the ministry of reconciliation; 19. To wit, that God was in Christ, reconciling the world unto himself, not imputing their trespasses unto them; and hath committed unto us the word of reconciliation.

God wants you so much that He wants your time, love, heart, body, spirit, soul, and companionship.

How about experiencing the real thing so you know how you are supposed to be treated. You will never get a woman or a man to give you all that God gave, but they should at least get halfway.

I guarantee you that once you pass the test of receiving and experiencing the love of God and companionship He wants to show you; then you will be ready for the one He will send you. God wants you to know what to look for by showing you the real thing so you don't get an imposter. If a woman never felt a real Louis Vuitton purse, she would be fooled by an imposter, and if a man never saw a real Rolex or cashmere overcoat he would be fooled by an imposter. You have to feel the real thing so you know what to look for in a man or woman.

2 Taming the Awakened Beast: "Controlling the Sex Drive"

Awaken is defined as to rouse or to excite to action from a state of idleness or from sleep.[2] Awaken also means to excite or revive something that seems dead.

Sex out of marriage is a spiritual demon that once awakened, will try to reign over you and drive you to sin, bad relationships, sexual diseases, one-night stands, feelings of unworthiness in church, and most of all it will destroy union with the Lord. The way the beast is awakened is just as the definition says: it is aroused from sleep. Being aroused entices one to wake up to a state of wanting action. In short terms you want to tap it or be tapped.

As a child the beast (sex) may have been awakened due to molestation, rape, an experienced boyfriend or girlfriend, pornography, young men or women touching themselves, or seeing someone having sex. All these awoke a part of your flesh and allowed the demonic spirit of lust or fornication to inhabit your body. In most, a strong sexual appetite is a generational curse passed down through the bloodline.

A beast is defined as something opposed to man or woman (something against you). It also means something irrational (not willing to reason or try to understand how another feels). A beast is something which pursues a course of life that destroys happiness.

Sex is an irrational beast. Once that joker is awakened, it does not reason or try to understand that you are trying to live right or get close to God. Its mentality (yes, I said mentality because it's "a spirit" and has a mind of its own) is I have to be fed, and I will do whatever, sometimes whoever, and, depending on how I feel, wherever I can so the job can get done.

Here are some Scriptures of people who were inhabited by demonic beings (similar to the sex spirit) and how they were out of control. Read Mark 5:1–13 where the writer Mark says,

> And they came over unto the other side of the sea, into the country of the Gadarenes. 2. And when he was come out of the ship, immediately there met him out of the tombs a man with an unclean spirit, 3. Who had his dwelling among the tombs; and *no man could bind him, no, not with chains:* 4. Because that he had been often bound with fetters and chains, and the chains had been plucked asunder by him, and the fetters broken in pieces: neither could any man tame him. 5. And always, night and day, he was in the mountains, and in the tombs, crying, and cutting himself with stones. 6. But when he saw Jesus afar off, *he ran and worshipped him*, 7. And cried with a

> loud voice, and said, What have I to do with thee, Jesus, thou Son of the most high God? I adjure thee by God, that thou torment me not. 8. For he said unto him, *Come out of the man, thou unclean spirit.* 9. And he asked him, What is thy name? And he answered, saying, *My name is Legion: for we are many.* 10. And he besought him much that he would not send them away out of the country. 11. Now there was there nigh unto the mountains a great herd of swine feeding. 12. And all the devils besought him, saying, Send us into the swine, that we may enter into them. 13. And forthwith Jesus gave them leave. And the unclean spirits went out, and entered into the swine: and the herd ran violently down a steep place into the sea, (they were about two thousand ;) and were choked in the sea.
>
> Mark 5:1–13 (emphasis added)

There were legions of devils in the man, which means over thousands of evil spirits. The evil spirit that reigned was the spirit of death. We know this because the demon loved to stay in the graveyard. There were legions of demons, but according to verse nine only one spake at first for them all. This gives us a spiritual understanding that a person can have many demons in them, but the one that is in charge or speaks is based on the place where the person is. The demon that is in control is in control only at the place where it is the strongest. For example an anger demon is in control at places where an individual gets angry the most. Demons have to feed, and the only way they can feed is if you take them to their place of habitation (place where they feel comfortable), so they can feed and get strong.

This is why the sex spirit, once it needs to get fed, will lead you to places like past relationships, strip clubs, illicit affairs, sex shops, your best friend's man or woman (oops), and places like that.

Another Scripture referring to demons is found in Mark 9:17–18, 20–27, where the writer Mark says,

> And one of the multitude answered and said, Master, I have brought unto thee my son, which hath a dumb spirit; And wheresoever he taketh him, he teareth him: and he foameth, and gnasheth with his teeth, and pineth away: and I spake to thy disciples 20. And they brought him unto him: and when he saw him, straightway the spirit tare him; and he fell on the ground, and wallowed foaming. 21. And he asked his father, How long is it ago since this came unto him? And he said, Of a child. 22. And ofttimes *it hath cast him into the fire, and into the waters, to destroy him: but if thou canst do any thing, have compassion on us, and help us.* Jesus said unto him, *If thou canst believe, all things are possible to him that believeth.* 24. And straightway the father of the child cried out, and said with tears, *Lord, I believe; help thou mine unbelief.* 25. When Jesus saw that the people came running together, he rebuked the foul spirit, saying unto him, Thou dumb and deaf spirit, I charge thee, come out of him, and enter no more into him. 26. And the spirit cried, and rent him sore, and came out of him: and he was as one dead; insomuch that many said, He is dead. 27. But Jesus took him by the hand, and lifted him up; and he arose.
>
> Mark 9:17–18, 20–27 (emphasis added)

According to verse twenty-two, this spirit was so strong in this boy that it tried to kill him. That sex spirit along with any evil spirit's job is to try to destroy you. The sex spirit will get you into a relationship with someone else who has the same spirit but also has AIDS. Its job is to take you out of here. One thing about this passage of Scripture that you must see is that any spirit can be cast out of you if you do three major things:

1. According to verse twenty-three—Believe that God can deliver you.
2. According to verse twenty-four—*Really* have a desire to want to be delivered (the father *cried out* for his son *with tears*).
3. According to verse twenty-five—Know that once you are sincere, it can be cast out today. Faith in God brings about an immediate deliverance.

Taming the Beast

The definition for the word *tame* is, to reduce from a *wild state* to a *domestic state*. It also means *to cage* (Like the character in Tyler Perry's movies Madea said, "clank clank") as to reduce the wildness and ferociousness. The word *tame* also means to subdue or to conquer by force or by a superior power in you, (Jesus Christ). The Apostle John writes in 1 John 4:4, "Ye are of God, little children, and have overcome them: because greater is he that is in you, than he that is in the world." The word *tame* also means to depress or put your foot on the head of that which you are taming. Luke 10:19 says "Behold, I give unto you power to tread on serpents and scorpions, and over all the power of the enemy: and nothing shall by any means hurt you." Finally, *tame* means to conquer or to fight the battle to win knowing it's already won. The writer Ezra says in 2 Chronicles 20:15b, "for the battle is not yours, but God's." The Apostle Paul also wrote in Romans 8:37, "Nay, in all these things we are more than conquerors through him that loved us."

If I am trying to tame a wild beast such as a lion, the first thing I must do is *take it out of its wild environment.* The only way you can tame and eventually kill that sex beast is you have to stop taking it to the places where it goes wild.

1 Thessalonians 5:22 says, "Abstain from all appearance of evil."

James 4:2–4 and 7 says,

> Ye lust, and have not: ye kill, and desire to have, and cannot obtain: ye fight and war, yet ye have not, because ye ask not. 3. Ye ask, and receive not, because ye ask amiss, that ye may consume it upon your lusts. 4. Ye adulterers and adulteresses, know ye not that the friendship of the world is enmity with God? whosoever therefore will be a friend of the world is the enemy of God. 7. Submit yourselves therefore to God. Resist the devil, and he will flee from you.

When you lust as a Christian for someone, God is not going to give them to you for good according to verse two. I pray you never try to kill somebody to get a man or woman. It's not that serious! Stop focusing on the flesh and focus on God.

The second thing I must do to tame and eventually kill a wild beast is to take it to a place where I can control it first. Most zoos take the beast from the jungle and put it in a fenced zoo and then a barred cage. The best way to tame the sex beast is to keep it in the house of God. Bible Study, prayer meeting, second Saturday meeting, Christian singles fellowship, Sunday Morning service, and Sunday School. What a zookeeper does is cage the beast so then he will be stronger and safe from its attack. When you do these things you put your *spirit man in position of strength* over your flesh and give it strength to overpower that demonic spirit of sex.

You are wrestling against devils who are trying to kill you. The Apostle John reminded us of the destiny of the devil and his crew in Revelation 20:10 which says, "And the devil that deceived them was cast into the lake of fire and brimstone, where the beast and the false prophet are, and shall be tormented day and night for ever and ever."

The devil knows that God cannot go back on His word. He knows Numbers 23:19 says, "God is not a man, that he should lie; neither the son of man, that he should repent: hath he said, and shall he not do it? or hath he spoken, and shall he not make it good?"

So then the devil knows that if you continue having sex then the prediction of Galatians 5:19 will occur, which says adultery and fornication are the works of the flesh, and then verse twenty-one says "they which do these things shall not inherit the kingdom of God."

God has to stick to His Word. In God's Word He says in 1 Corinthians 7:9, "But if they cannot contain, let them marry: for it is better to marry than to burn."

The blessing for us though is God made a way for us to get back in good standing with Him. The Apostle John says in 1 John 1:9 and 2:1,

> "If we confess our sins, he is faithful and just to forgive us our sins, and to cleanse us from all unrighteousness. My little children, these things write I unto you, that ye sin not. And if any man sin, we have an advocate with the Father, Jesus Christ the righteous."

This does not mean that every time you want to knock boots you can just do it and ask for forgiveness. That is why God added Hebrews 10:26, which says, "For if we sin willfully after that we have received the knowledge of the truth, there remaineth no more sacrifice for sins."

Last but not least, another way to *tame* the wild beast sex is just like the zoo says *don't feed or touch the animals.* You have to stop feeding that sex demon [no sex on TV, sex magazines, phone sex, sex shops, nibbling on the ears (it always leads to more), hugs, and finally sex toys are just as bad (vibrators, plastic dildos, and fake vaginas)]. *You know all bases have to be covered.* Leave no room for the enemy to say, "They didn't say you couldn't do this."

Here are some Scriptures to remember:

1. Matthew 7:18–19

A good tree cannot bring forth evil fruit, neither can a corrupt tree bring forth good fruit. 19. Every tree that bringeth not forth good fruit is hewn down, and cast into the fire.

2. Romans 1:28–29

And even as they did not like to retain God in their knowledge, God gave them over to a reprobate mind, to do those things which are not convenient; 29. Being filled with all unrighteousness, fornication.

3. 1 Corinthians 7:9

But if they cannot contain, let them marry: for it is better to marry than to burn.

4. Galatians 5:17,19

For the flesh lusteth against the Spirit, and the Spirit against the flesh: and these are contrary the one to the other: so that ye cannot do the things that ye would. 19. Now the works of the flesh are manifest, which are these; adultery, fornication.

5. Colossians 3:5

Mortify therefore your members which are upon the earth; fornication, uncleanness, inordinate affection, evil concupiscence, and covetousness, which is idolatry: [Stop coveting someone else's man or woman because that is idolatry]

3 Loneliness

Do you feel lonely? Don't you deserve companionship? Everyone else seems to have someone but you. You say, "I am tired of coming home to an empty house or bedroom." If you have children, then you say "I need someone who I can have an adult conversation with or someone who I can relate to."

You say as a woman, "Pastor, I need security because I don't like coming home and wondering if I'm gonna get attacked." You say as a man, "Pastor, I need to come home and have someone to make me feel like a man." My brothers and sisters, let's break down the word loneliness and find out scripturally why God wants you lonely for now.

Are you ready? This will change your whole perception on being lonely.

First, let's define loneliness. Loneliness is defined as without human companionship, isolated, being the only one of its kind (distinct), and unfrequented by people or receiving few or no visitors.

Well let's break down each part of this definition.

1. Without human companionship

Why would God leave me without human companionship for this season of my life? Well the word *companionship* means one employed to aid, live with, and accompany another. It also means a matched pair or set. Sometimes your immediate expectancy for companionship is not God's ordained time for you to have companionship.

Human companionship in many cases leads to human reliance. Human companionship leads to less companionship with the Lord. God keeps us without human companionship also because most of us, once we get a man or woman, are in so much of a rush to lock and chain them because we don't want to lose them and become lonely all over again. So we make the mistake of sometimes settling for the wrong man or woman and try to rush into a deep relationship with them before we hear God say "They ain't the one," and we have to let them go. Most times we know they aren't the one God wants us to be with because the signs are all there, but because our desire to not be lonely is so strong, we become blind to the signs. Eventually, God makes that man or woman leave us or hurt us to get us to let them go, because we wouldn't let them go and they were no good for us. (*You know what I'm talking about. Think of one relationship God saved you from that you thought was good for you then, but now after looking back over it you would've went crazy or even been killed if you would've stayed there.*)

The Apostle Paul writes to us in 1 Corinthians 7:32, 34,

> But I would have you without carefulness. He that is *unmarried careth for the things that belong to the Lord,*

> *how he may please the Lord:* 34. There is difference also between a wife and a virgin. *The unmarried woman careth for the things of the Lord, that she may be holy both in body and in spirit*: but she that is married careth for the things of the world, how she may please her husband.
>
> 1 Corinthians 7:32, 34 (emphasis added)

Paul tells us that when you are married or have human companionship, your focus turns from pleasing God to pleasing that man or woman in your life. One thing that God show us over and over again is that the reason why He keeps us without is so He can come within.

Single man, single woman, *God wants you.* Let me say that one more time because you didn't hear me, *God wants you.* There are some folks He allows to get married because His will was to let them move on, but for some strange reason He really wants you to Himself. Paul said the unmarried careth for the things of the Lord, how they may please Him. So the reason I have no human companionship is because God wants me to focus on pleasing Him.

So then, I am not really alone because I have learned that the Creator of the whole world has a personal interest of intimacy for me. He desires a worshipper. Read John 4:23: "But the hour cometh, and now is when the true worshippers shall worship the Father in spirit and in truth: for the Father seeketh for such to worship Him." He is desperately looking for someone who wants only intimacy with Him.

He wants me to have a *mountain top* experience with Him. This means I have to be alone with Him.

Read Genesis 32:22–30—God wants intimacy with you

to change the fears in your life into assurance that He will never leave you.

God's is looking for those whose main focus is to please Him by worshipping Him. This worship brings you into intimacy with God to where the need for human companionship becomes null and void. (Some of you know what I am talking about). This is because once you get into His presence you don't want any man or woman trying to tell you when and how often you can have your time with God.

According to 1 Corinthians 7:33–34b, the married care for the things of their spouse to please them. So their focus is more for their spouse than for God. Did you know that *there are married folk who have human companions, but are still lonely*? Being married doesn't guarantee you won't be lonely. Most have learned that being married doesn't mean you are not going to be lonely.

I guess that is why fifty percent of marriages end in divorce these days. Before I get tied down with any human companionship, I want to feel God's companionship first so just in case the man or woman leaves me or I have to leave them, I won't be devastated because I learned beforehand how to get intimate with God first.

Are you a seeker of God? Moses writes in Deuteronomy 4:29–31,

> But if from thence thou shalt seek the Lord thy God, thou shalt find him, if thou seek him with all thy heart and with all thy soul. 30. When thou art in tribulation, and all these things are come upon thee, even in the latter days, if thou turn to the Lord thy God, and shalt be obedient unto his voice; 31. (For

> the Lord thy God is a merciful God;) he will not forsake thee, neither destroy thee, nor forget the covenant of thy fathers which he sware unto them.
>
> Deuteronomy 4:29–31

As a single person, you ought to have such a deep relationship with God because you learn that as Deuteronomy 4:29–30 says, if you seek Him with your whole heart and soul not only will you find Him but when you get into trouble and all troubles are weighing you down He will not forsake you or leave you. I learned the hard way that when times are good everybody wants to be with you, but when they get tough no one is there then.

Others may leave you alone sometimes, but the Lord is always there.

Psalm 9:10 says "And they that know thy name will put their trust in thee: for thou, Lord, hast not forsaken them that seek thee."

Psalms 27:8–10 says:

> When thou saidst, *Seek ye my face; my heart said unto thee, Thy face, Lord, will I seek.* 9. Hide not thy face far from me; put not thy servant away in anger: thou hast been my help; leave me not, neither forsake me, O God of my salvation. 10. *When my father and my mother forsake me, then the Lord will take me up.*
>
> Psalm 27:8–10 (emphasis added)

Sometimes in loneliness you cry because you feel no one is there or no one cares, but in that moment seek your First Love. You will learn how to praise your way out of trouble into triumph. Psalms 42:1–5 tells us how to seek after God by saying,

> As the hart panteth after the water brooks, so panteth my soul after thee, O God. 2. My soul thirsteth for God, for the living God: when shall I come and appear before God? 3. *My tears have been my meat day and night, while they continually say unto me, Where is thy God?* 4. When I remember these things, I pour out my soul in me: for I had gone with the multitude, *I went with them to the house of God, with the voice of joy and praise,* with a multitude that kept holyday. 5. Why art thou cast down, O my soul? and why art thou disquieted in me? Hope thou in God: for I shall yet praise him for the help of his countenance.
>
> Psalm 42:1–5 (emphasis added)

If you seek Him early the rest of the day, He will walk with you and you won't feel alone.

Psalm 63:1, says "O God, thou art my God; early will I seek thee: my soul thirsteth for thee, my flesh longeth for thee in a dry and thirsty land, where no water is." Hebrews 11:6 says "But without faith it is impossible to please *him*: for he that cometh to God must believe that he is, and *that* he is a rewarder of them that diligently seek him." *God separates me to bless me!* Job 19:13–19 says,

> He has put my family far from me, and my acquaintances are wholly estranged from me. 14. My *relatives and my close friends have failed me*; 15. The guests in my house have forgotten me; my serving girls count me as a stranger; I have become an alien

> in their eyes. 16. I call to my servant, but he gives me no answer; I must myself plead with him. 17. My breath is repulsive to my wife; I am loathsome to my own family. 18. Even young children despise me; when I rise, they talk against me. 19. All my intimate friends abhor me, and those whom I loved have turned against me.
>
> Job 19:13–19 (emphasis added)

Sometimes God allows you to go through loneliness to show you who really will be there until the end. Everyone else walks out on you when there's no benefit for them, but God walks in to give benefit to you.

2. *Loneliness* also means isolated

Why would God want me isolated from others? Isolation is something that causes you to focus on something or someone other than the place of your isolation.

In prison or jail if an inmate acts up, the guard puts them into an isolation cell for days, weeks, and sometimes months. If that prisoner doesn't focus on something that will occupy his mind, instead of focusing on the place where he has been placed he will crack or lose his mind.

So then God does the same thing with us. My loneliness or isolation makes me focus on something else to fill the void in my life. Some people fill it with by working overtime, working out, taking eighteen hours in college while working, worrying all night, focusing on bad relationships that they sit and weep about. God isolated you to get your mind on Him *so He can finally give you peace in your life.* Isaiah 26:3 says,

"Thou wilt keep him in perfect peace, whose mind is stayed on thee: because he trusteth in thee." So to overcome loneliness, keep your mind on God. He will keep you in perfect peace. There's no peace and serenity like that of God.

Loneliness also means being the only one of your kind or distinct. I know sometimes you feel like you're the only one without somebody. You have thought it was a curse or that other people were lucky or blessed. You felt God must have it out for you, or that He is mad at you. I come to let you know that it's *quite* the *opposite*. He is showing your distinction from others who need people to make them feel complete, to you who are complete by yourself in God.

You always thought that married folk had it all together. Most married folk needed companions to make them feel complete, but you have been made distinct to prove to everyone in your life that Jesus Christ has made you complete. When it is my time to have someone, I will already be complete before God gives her to me. No more hurt, pain, low self-esteem, abuse, lack of trust issues, etc. because my time with God has healed all my bruises and wounds and now I can go into a relationship not making the new man or woman pay for the mistakes the past man or woman did to me.

Say this: I am fearfully and wonderfully made in the image of God, and with or without a man or woman I still got it going on. You have to make married people envy you instead of you always envying them.

I am a God chaser. I don't have time to chase anyone I have to try to kill myself to keep. My heart is fixed, and my mind is made up that I'm going to pour myself into the

Lord. Colossians 2:10 says, "*And ye are complete in him*, which is the head of all principality and power" (emphasis added).

You don't need anyone to make you feel complete. You are already complete in Christ. God is making a distinction between the "wanna be" and the "gotta be." I gotta be his love. John 14:17 says "Even the *Spirit of truth*; whom the world cannot receive, because it seeth him not, neither knoweth him: but ye know him; *for he dwelleth with you, and shall be in you*" (emphasis added).

He wants to be within you. Paul writes in 1 Corinthians 6:17–20,

> But he that is joined unto the Lord is one spirit. 18. *Flee fornication. Every sin that a man doeth is without the body; but he that committeth fornication sinneth against his own body.* 19. What? know ye not that *your body is the temple of the Holy Ghost which is in you, which ye have of God, and ye are not your own?* 20. For ye are bought with a price: therefore glorify God in your body, and in your spirit, which are God's."
>
> 1 Corinthians 6:17–20 (emphasis added)

God wants to teach you in your loneliness how to be a man or woman, a father or mother, and a Christian. Some of us did not have parents or mentors to teach us how to be great. God wants you to be taught only by Him. In that teaching there will also be some healing, because you cannot go into a new relationship with old baggage. If you weren't alone, you wouldn't have the time to be taught because you would have to focus on someone else. In most relationships today, the other party has to spend time now to not only help heal the other, but also sometimes teach the other how to be a real man or woman. Let God have time to *heal your hurt, change your way of thinking, make you whole, and teach you to love yourself first* at this season of your life.

Finally, loneliness means unfrequented by people or having few or no visitors. You may have been bitter or are bitter with the fact that currently you are so alone that you wish anybody would come and even visit you. God, can you send me someone just to go out with and have fun? Can you send me someone just to chill with? My brother and sister, God knows you. Psalms 139:1–4 says,

> O Lord, thou hast searched me, and known me. 2. Thou knowest my downsitting and mine uprising, thou understandest my thought afar off. 3. Thou compassest my path and my lying down, and art acquainted with all my ways. 4. For there is not a word in my tongue, but, lo, O Lord, thou knowest it altogether.

You may say, I'll just hang with them, but God knows that once you get attached to anyone, your focus will be off of Him to do things with them. Again do not forget that you are at a season of personal spiritual growth and the longer you prolong the growth by spending time with people other than God, the longer before you go to the next level. That even means stop focusing so much on that child who's over eighteen-years-old, *it's your time now*!

Also know that once you get closer to God, you get further from people who don't want to get closer to God. So it's not that people do not like you, but it's just that you are carrying a higher anointing now that just anybody can't just hang with you. If you read Luke 6:22–23, it says,

> Blessed are ye, when men shall hate you, and when they shall separate you from their company, and shall reproach you, and cast out your name as evil, for the Son of man's sake. 23. Rejoice ye in that day, and leap for joy: for, behold, your reward is great in heaven.

Your anointing is a conviction to some and definitely a devil rebuker to others.

You may lose human visitors in being one with God, but you gain the Great Visitor. Philippians 3:8 says, "Yea doubtless, and I count all things but loss for the excellency of the knowledge of Christ Jesus my Lord: for whom I have suffered the loss of all things, and do count them but dung, that I may win Christ."

Once we learn that God is separating us to teach us to love and trust Him first, then we can move to the next level and have companionship with others without the fear of losing them. This is because we know if we lose them we have assurance that we always have God, our first Love.

Single man or woman, don't trip. God is preparing you in this loneliness or isolation for great things. Great men and women are those who have intimacy with the great God and Lord Jesus Christ.

God is preparing great things for you this year. Are you ready, or are you going to continue focusing on being alone? You're not alone; you have God. He's your *provider, sustainer, promise keeper, lover, protector*, and everything else you need.

4 Struggling Financially

Struggling financially is something that almost everyone at one time in their lives has had to deal with. To struggle financially does not mean you have to be broke; it can also mean you have to deal with day to day struggles to maintain a certain lifestyle.

Being single and trying to maintain today's quote unquote successful lifestyle is hard with just one income coming in. In today's society it usually takes dual incomes to survive. Most married households need both husband and wife to work in order to sometimes just make it. Somehow and some way you have maintained shelter, food, and clothing for yourself and even children by yourself. Well I wonder who took care of making sure you didn't go crazy doing it.

Did you know that incomes from a government-assistance income to a president-of-a-firm income are all provided by God? God determines who is promoted and blessed according to Psalms 75:6–7. The Scripture says, "For promotion cometh neither from the east, nor from the west, nor from the south. But God is the judge: he putteth down one, and setteth up another."

This Scripture teaches us that in each job or promotion you receive, God is the one that provided the opportunity.

The word *struggle* means to contend against, compete with, or to progress or penetrate with difficulty. I know that we have all had to face all these just to make it this far, but the question I want to ask you is through your struggling, competing, and difficulty did you at anytime wonder how it always somehow and some way came together.

Well let's look at Scripture and find out how it happened. Matthew 7:7–11 reads,

> Ask, and it shall be given you; seek, and ye shall find; knock and it shall be opened unto you: 8. For every one that asketh receiveth; and he that seeketh findeth; and to him that knocketh it shall be opened. 9. Or what man is there of you, whom if his son ask bread, will he give him a stone? 10. Or if he ask a fish, will he give him a serpent? 11. If ye then, being evil, know how to give good gifts unto your children, how much more shall your Father which is in heaven give good things to them that ask him?

God is a good Father and provider, and yes, He cares. Ask for it, and He will show up. Psalm 84:11 tells us, "For the Lord God is a sun and shield: the Lord will give grace and glory: no good thing will he withhold from them that walk uprightly."

I know it is sometimes hard to do right, but man or woman of God, if you follow and obey God's Word and commandment He will fulfill His promise to provide all your needs. Stop letting the devil rob you of your blessings. Stop letting illicit affairs and sin stop your overflow of blessings. Look at Jeremiah 5:24–25 where the Lord tells us,

> Neither say they in their heart, Let us now fear the Lord our God, that giveth rain, both the former and the latter, in his season: he reserveth unto us the appointed weeks of the harvest. 25. Your iniquities have turned away these things, and your sins have withholden good things from you.

(Read verse twenty-five again)

Sin is the main thing that stops your blessings. Repent (turn away from it) and be blessed.

As of today, I want you to stop stressing on if God will help you in tough times financially. Number 23:19 says, "God is not a man that he should lie; neither the son of man that he should repent: hath he said, and shall he not do it? or hath he spoken, and shall he not make it good?"

When God's Word says something, He has to make it happen.

Read Psalm 55:22 which says, "Cast thy burden upon the Lord, and he shall sustain thee: he shall never suffer the righteous to be moved." Also check out Psalms 3:1–5: which promises you,

> Lord, how they are increased that trouble me! Many are they that rise up against me. 2. Many there be which say of my soul, There is no help for him in God. Selah. 3. But thou, O Lord, art a shield for me; my glory, and the lifter up of mine head. 4. I cried

> unto the Lord with my voice, and he heard me out of his holy hill. Selah. 5. I laid me down and slept; I awaked; for the Lord sustained me.

Verse one of Psalm 3 says "How are they increased." Sometimes bills and collectors increase around you and trouble you, but child of God, I want you to hope in God now. Verse two says they (collectors and bills) say to you as well as the devil, "There is no help for you in God." They tell you to give up hope and worry, but verse three gives us the true answer. Verse three tells us that when the devil tells you to give up, you need to give a response. The key is not to respond negatively, but respond by reminding God of His Word.

David said in verse three, "But thou O Lord art a shield for me (about me) my glory: and the lifter up of mine head."

God not only will be the shield to not allow all the arrows of financial struggle to shoot and kill you, but He also is the lifter up of your head. God says don't drop your head when it gets hard and you feel hopeless. God is gonna lift your head so you can look up to the place or to the One who will provide for you. Psalms 24:7–10 says,

> Lift up your heads, O ye gates; and be ye lift up, ye everlasting doors; and the King of glory shall come in. 8. Who is this King of glory? The Lord strong and mighty, the Lord mighty in battle. 9. Lift up your heads, O ye gates; even lift them up, ye everlasting doors; and the King of glory shall come in. 10. Who is this King of glory? The Lord of hosts, he is the King of glory. Selah.

The psalmist tells us, "Lift up your Head" to see the King of Glory coming. Help is on the way; Jesus is coming to deliver you from your distress and troubles. Also if you lift your head, you can be like the psalmist in Psalm 121:1–8 when he said,

> I Will lift up mine eyes unto the hills, from whence cometh my help. 2. My help cometh from the Lord, which made heaven and earth. 3. He will not suffer thy foot to be moved: he that keepeth thee will not slumber. 4. Behold, he that keepeth Israel shall neither slumber nor sleep. 5. The Lord is thy keeper: the Lord is thy shade upon thy right hand. 6. The sun shall not smite thee by day, nor the moon by night. 7. The Lord shall preserve thee from all evil: he shall preserve thy soul. 8. The Lord shall preserve thy going out and thy coming in from this time forth, and even for evermore.

How Do I Overcome Financial Struggle?

First to overcome it, you must change the way you think. Is it ever a struggle when you have a guarantee it will be met?

Now before we go forward, remember to be a good steward over what God gives you. Learn how to budget and not overspend. Then remember God has given us promises that we need to walk in. Philippians 4:19 says, "But my God shall supply all your need according to his riches in glory by Christ Jesus." Psalm 23: 1 claims, "The Lord is my shepherd; I shall not want." In Matthew 6:25–34 Jesus tells us:

> "Therefore I say unto you, *Take no thought for your*

> *life, what ye shall eat, or what ye shall drink; nor yet for your body, what ye shall put on. Is not the life more than meat, and the body than raiment?* 26. Behold the fowls of the air: for they sow not, neither do they reap, nor gather into barns; yet your heavenly Father feedeth them. Are ye not much better than they? 27. Which of you by taking thought can add one cubit unto his stature? 28. And why take ye thought for raiment? Consider the lilies of the field, how they grow; they toil not, neither do they spin: 29. And yet I say unto you, That even Solomon in all his glory was not arrayed like one of these. 30. Wherefore, if God so clothe the grass of the field, which to day is, and to morrow is cast into the oven, shall he not much more clothe you, O ye of little faith? 31. *Therefore take no thought, saying, What shall we eat? or, What shall we drink? or, Wherewithal shall we be clothed?* 32. (For after all these things do the Gentiles seek:) *for your heavenly Father knoweth that ye have need of all these things.* 33. But seek ye first the kingdom of God, and his righteousness; and all these things shall be added unto you. 34. *Take therefore no thought for the morrow: for the morrow shall take thought for the things of itself. Sufficient unto the day is the evil thereof.*"
>
> Matthew 6:25–34 (emphasis added)

I got one more for you; are you ready? Look at Deuteronomy 28:1–14 which promises,

> And it shall come to pass, if thou shalt hearken diligently unto the voice of the Lord thy God, to observe and to do all his commandments which I command thee this day, that the Lord thy God will

set thee on high above all nations of the earth: 2. And all these blessings shall come on thee, and overtake thee, if thou shalt hearken unto the voice of the Lord thy God. 3. Blessed shalt thou be in the city, and blessed shalt thou be in the field. 4. Blessed shall be the fruit of thy body, and the fruit of thy ground, and the fruit of thy cattle, the increase of thy kine, and the flocks of thy sheep. 5. Blessed shall be thy basket and thy store. 6. Blessed shalt thou be when thou comest in, and blessed shalt thou be when thou goest out. 7. The Lord shall cause thine enemies that rise up against thee to be smitten before thy face: they shall come out against thee one way, and flee before thee seven ways. 8. The Lord shall command the blessing upon thee in thy storehouses, and in all that thou settest thine hand unto; and he shall bless thee in the land which the Lord thy God giveth thee. 9. The Lord shall establish thee an holy people unto himself, as he hath sworn unto thee, if thou shalt keep the commandments of the Lord thy God, and walk in his ways. 10. And all people of the earth shall see that thou art called by the name of Lord; and they shall be afraid of thee. 11. And the Lord shall make thee plenteous in goods, in the fruit of thy body, and in the fruit of thy cattle, and in the fruit of thy ground, in the land which the Lord sware unto thy fathers to give thee. 12. The Lord shall open unto thee his good treasure, the heaven to give the rain unto thy land in his season, and to bless all the work of thine hand: and thou shalt lend unto many nations, and thou shalt not borrow. 13. And the Lord shall make thee the head, and not the tail; and thou shalt be above only, and thou shalt not be beneath;

> if that thou hearken unto the commandments of the Lord thy God, which I command thee this day, to observe and to do them: 14. And thou shalt not go aside from any of the words which I command thee this day, to the right hand, or to the left, to go after other gods to serve them.

You may have to suffer for a while, but that is to teach you to trust God. Read 1 Peter 5:10 which says, "But the God of all grace, who hath called us unto his eternal glory by Christ Jesus, *after that ye have suffered a while, make you perfect, stablish, strengthen, settle you.*"

After your struggle God is gonna perfect or mature you, establish you (set you up to not be moved), strengthen you (give you strength to be strong for the coming storms), and settle you (put you in a sure place, with sure provision, and sure confidence).

When God blesses you, you don't have to apologize for being blessed because it was the Lord that did it.

Another way to overcome financial struggle is to break the generational curse of lack from your life. Once you accept Jesus Christ into your life, you automatically have the power to break the curse off your life.

Second Corinthians 5:17 says, "Therefore if any man be in Christ, he is a new creature: old things are passed away; behold all things are become new."

When you become new that means your life is now hid in Christ and all the curses on your life are broken.

Verse twenty tells us, "Now then we are ambassadors for Christ." To be an ambassador of Christ means you live as a direct representative of Christ. In the government system when a country sends an ambassador to another country, they have to pay off all their bills, provide housing, and meet all their needs. It is a discredit for the country to have an ambassador in lack. In the same way, as Christ ambassadors it is a discredit to God to have His own in lack.

Financially Successful Singles

First of all God has given you a way of achieving a financially successful life that supersedes any investment or worldly way of making money. Now carnally minded people won't understand or appreciate this way, but when you are God's child you have to follow His ways. Just like any parent when your child disobeys you, you don't award them with an allowance. God can't award you when you don't use His principles. First Corinthians 2:9–10, 14–15 says,

> But as it is written, Eye hath not seen, nor ear heard, neither have entered into the heart of man, the things which God hath prepared for them that love him. But God hath revealed them unto us by his Spirit: for the Spirit searcheth all things, yea, the deep things of God. 14. But the natural man receiveth not the things of the Spirit of God: for they are foolishness unto him: neither can he know them, because they are spiritually discerned. 15. But he that is spiritual judgeth all things, yet he himself is judged of no man.

Are you ready to move from *financial struggle to financial success*? Then use these following principles:

Principle #1 — Sow your way out of debt!

2 Corinthians 9:6–11 reads:

> But this I say, He which soweth sparingly shall reap also sparingly; and he which soweth bountifully shall reap also bountifully. [If you sow to bless the Kingdom of God you will reap abundantly.] 7. Every man according as he purposeth in his heart, so let him give; not grudgingly [not wanting to really give], or of necessity [because you want something in return]: for God loveth a cheerful giver [a giver who loves God and His people, and wants to see the Kingdom of God go further]. 8. And God is able to make all grace abound toward you [If you do verse seven, God will give favor to you, and it will abound.]; that ye, always having all sufficiency in all things, may abound to every good work: 9. (As it is written, He hath dispersed abroad; he hath given to the poor: his righteousness remaineth for ever.10. Now he that ministereth seed to the sower both minister bread for your food, and multiply your seed sown, and increase the fruits of your righteousness;) 11. Being enriched in every thing to all bountifulness [everything in your life will be blessed], which causeth through us thanksgiving to God.

Also to go along with this principle Galatians 6:7–10 says

> Be not deceived; God is not mocked: for whatsoever a man soweth, that shall he also reap. [Whatever you plant you will reap!] 8. For he that soweth to his flesh shall of the flesh reap corruption; but he that soweth

> to the Spirit shall of the Spirit reap life everlasting. 9. And let us not be weary in well doing: for in due season we shall reap, if we faint not. [When the harvest tarries, know God cannot lie] 10. As we have therefore opportunity, let us do good unto all men, especially unto them who are of the household of faith.

Principle #2—Try to out-give God

Isaiah 55:10b tells us that God gives seed to the sower. You don't have seed or money because when God blessed you with it before, you ate up your seed instead of sowing it. If you plant a seed it will bring a harvest (more than enough) to you, but if you eat the seed no *harvest* will come. Genesis 8:22 says, "God says while the Earth remain there will be seedtime and harvest." While you are here if you want a harvest, plant a seed!

Principle #3—Stay Obedient

It is easy to start a New Year resolution or start something, but only a strong person can stay consistent come hell or high water. Malachi 3:8–12 says if you stay consistent this will happen:

> Will a man rob God? Yet ye have robbed me. But ye say, Wherein have we robbed thee? In tithes and offerings. 9. Ye are cursed with a curse (God can not lie): for ye have robbed me, even this whole nation. 10. Bring ye all the tithes into the storehouse, that there may be meat in mine house, and prove me now herewith, saith the Lord of hosts, if I will not

> open you the windows of heaven, and pour you out a blessing, that there shall not be room enough to receive it. (Sounds like a promise to me) 11. And I will rebuke the devourer for your sakes, and he shall not destroy the fruits of your ground; neither shall your vine cast her fruit before the time in the field, saith the Lord of hosts. (Sounds like He will protect your investment) 12. And all nations shall call you blessed: for ye shall be a delightsome land, saith the Lord of hosts."

Then Haggai 1:4–11 tells us how God's people start but then slack off. When this happens God says the following will occur:

> Is it time for you, O ye, to dwell in your ceiled houses, and this house lie waste? [Taking care of your priorities and leaves God's house without] 5. Now therefore thus saith the Lord of hosts; Consider your ways. 6. Ye have sown much, and bring in little; ye eat, but ye have not enough; ye drink, but ye are not filled with drink; ye clothe you, but there is none warm; and he that earneth wages earneth wages to put it into a bag with holes. 7. Thus saith the Lord of hosts; Consider your ways. 8. Go up to the mountain, and bring wood, and build the house; and I will take pleasure in it, and I will be glorified, saith the Lord. 9. Ye looked for much, and, lo it came to little; and when ye brought it home, I did blow upon it. [God said you brought home income, groceries, etc. but it was consumed so fast] Why? saith the Lord of hosts. Because of mine house that is waste, and ye run every man unto his own house. 10. Therefore the

> heaven over you is stayed from dew, and the earth is stayed from her fruit. [God said, "I shut up your blessing and closed the door."] 11. And I called for a drought upon the land, and upon the mountains, and upon the corn, and upon the new wine, and upon the oil, and upon that which the ground bringeth forth, and upon men, and upon cattle, and upon all the labour of the hands."

Now watch this: if you are broke and stressed financially, give God's Word an opportunity. If you are watching people who do not tithe and are financially doing fine, remember Hebrews 12:6, 8 which says, "For whom the Lord loveth he chasteneth, and scourgeth every son whom he receiveth. But if ye be without chastisement, whereof all are partakers, then are ye bastards, and not sons." The reason why you keep getting whopped is because you are His.

Principle #4—Don't be lazy

To overcome financial struggle, get off your lazy seat and get out there and make it happen. Get yourself to a place to be blessed. Poverty is for the sluggard, or lazy person. Proverbs 6:6–11 tells us about the lazy person by saying,

> Go to the ant, thou sluggard; consider her ways, and be wise: 7. Which having no guide, overseer, or ruler [nobody stayed on them to work], 8. Provideth her meat in the summer, and gathereth her food in the harvest. 9. How long wilt thou sleep, O sluggard? When wilt thou arise out of thy sleep? 10. Yet a little sleep, a little slumber, a little folding of the hands

> to sleep: 11. So shall thy poverty come as one that travelleth, and thy want as an armed man.

Remember, use your hands and go out there and get your blessing. Ecclesiastes 9:10 says "Whatsoever thy hand findeth to do, do it with thy might; for there is no work, nor device, nor knowledge, nor wisdom, in the grave, whither thou goest." In other words don't die and then say "I wish I would have done this or that."

Know to gather your harvest when it's ripe and do not sit around and miss your season for blessing.

Proverbs 10:4–5 says,

> He becometh poor that dealeth with a slack hand: but the hand of the diligent maketh rich. He that gathereth in summer is a wise son: but he that sleepeth in harvest is a son that causeth shame.

God wants to bless you, but to receive the blessings of God you have to get up in the morning and work.

Proverbs 20:13 says, "Love not sleep, lest thou come to poverty; open thine eyes, and thou shalt be satisfied with bread."

To walk in financial success, stop hanging around people who want to lay in, play play station, watch soap operas , or just plain lay around and choose not to work. There's even a Scripture that tells us to stop hanging around lazy people. Proverbs 12:11 says, "He that tilleth his land shall be satisfied with bread: but he that followeth lazy persons is void of understanding."

Staying Financially Successful

To stay financially successful I want you to remember three very important principles. Principle one is when God blesses you, don't forget who blessed you and remember to praise God, for it is He who blessed you. Many people cry to God for help, and once they are helped they forget the helper and use words like "I got here on my own." God warns us of this in Deuteronomy 8: 16–17:

> And thou say in thine heart, My power and the might of mine hand hath gotten me this wealth. But thou shalt remember the Lord thy God: for it is he that giveth thee power to get wealth.

The second principle is when God blesses you, do not misuse the blessing. Be a good steward or overseer over what God has given you. Child of God do not let those new-found friends get you to spend your money on things that are not equity building. You will so find out that as soon as people see God blessing you, they will want to hang with you; and just as soon as you are without money, you are without friends. Proverbs 19:4 proves this by saying, "Wealth maketh many friends; but the poor is separated from his neighbor."

The third principle is don't keep money at places where it is accessible for you to get to whenever you want it. If spending money is your hang up, then the more accessible it is, the greater the chance you will spend it. I want you to put your excess money (yes, I did say excess because if you follow the above principles God is getting ready to bless you beyond your imagination). Ephesians 3:20 says it this way: "Now unto him that is able to do exceeding abundantly above all that we ask or think, according to the power [your faith] that worketh in us." Put that excess into a mutual fund, annuity, or savings account where there is a penalty charged if you try to withdraw it. This will discourage you from withdrawing your money. I also want you to start investing your money in real estate or some other type of solid investment that will yield you a sizable return.

Go for it!

5

Learning What to Lose in Order to Gain

Single man or single woman, I want you to say this after me. Are you ready?

Say, "I am so blessed and favored that if you are not going to where God is taking me you might want to get off at the next stop." There are some people and things in your life, man or woman of God, that you are gonna have to let go of before you go to the next level in God. We have to learn what to lose in order to gain. In other words you have to know what weight in your life is stopping you from going higher in God. Are you ready? Hebrews 12:1–2 says,

> Wherefore seeing we also are compassed about with so great a cloud of witnesses, let us lay aside every weight, and the sin which doth so easily beset us, and let us run with patience the race that is set before us, Looking unto Jesus the author and finisher of our faith; who for the joy that was set before him

> endured the cross, despising the shame, and is set down at the right hand of the throne of God.

As we break down this Scripture I want you to be attentive to the blessings of dropping unneeded baggage so you can take a higher and greater flight in God. Hebrews 12:1 says, "Wherefore seeing also." Now stop right there because whenever you see the word *also* you need to seek what preceded the current verse. Then we have to go to Hebrews 11:37–40 which says,

> They were stoned, they were sawn asunder, were tempted, were slain with the sword: they wandered about in sheepskins and goatskins; being destitute, afflicted, tormented; 38. (Of whom the world was not worthy:) they wandered in deserts, and in mountains, and in dens and caves of the earth. 39. And these all, having obtained a good report through faith, received not the promise: 40. God having provided some better thing for us, that they without us should not be made perfect.

These saints went through trials, tribulations, death, and homelessness and didn't obtain the promises and blessings that we are receiving now because Jesus Christ had not yet come and bestowed the blessings on them. We on the other hand have a blessing as Hebrews 11:40 says: "God having provided some better thing for us." The key to this Scripture is that the old saints went through the extreme pain, and we are receiving the extreme prosperity. So the writer says since God decided to provide a better thing for us, we need to do the following. Hebrews 12:1 says "let us lay aside every weight, and the sin that so easily beset us or catches us up." The Greek word for lay aside is *apotithemi*—which means to put away, cast off, lay apart from, lay down, and put away. God told me to tell you, man or woman of God, that He is not just ready but willing to raise you out of the struggles, hardship, pain, and lack of confidence; but the only way you can get to *the place* that God has set up for you is to have a *loss* in order to receive a *gain.*

The writer says lay aside—cast it off, step out of your grave clothes. In Isaiah 61:3, Isaiah writes a prophetic word for you that the Lord Jesus will perform in your life. He said He would give you the garment of praise for the spirit of heaviness. God said when you cast off that weight and sin that you know is keeping you grounded without the ability to rise, cast it off and then God will give you a change of spiritual clothes. (*He's gonna give you praise instead of heaviness*). As you are reading this now, it has already happened. That heaviness and weight you have been carrying, God just set you free. Now I want you to put on your garment of praise and bless God right now for the release of the weight. (*I don't know where you are reading this book, but go ahead and let God know how you are not ashamed to praise him.*)

Now you may be asking me, pastor, what is the weight I am carrying. Well let's define *weight. Weight* is defined as a gravitational force exerted by another object or body equal to the product of the other object or bodies mass. In other words a weight is something or someone who tries to keep you at the same weight they are so you stay at the same level they are. You, man of God and woman of God, have something Satan has sent into your life to keep you at the same level you've been at for a while. I don't care what it is; if it is some sin, get it out; it is robbing you. If it is a person, get them out; they are weighing you down. *Weight* also is defined as an object used to hold something down. You are in a relationship where the other party is not trying to grow closer to God nor are they trying to grow out of the norm to the supernatural. All they want is what you can do for them, but what have they done for you lately? I am so glad that God moved some of the women out of my life who I had to work hard to try to impress and keep when all they wanted was what I could give them and not what they could give me. God said let it go, and let it go I did; and as soon as I got rid of the loss, I immediately got the gain.

I know you are saying, Pastor, if I let go of the one that I am holding on to even though I know God is not pleased with it and how I am living, I lose security and quite a few other things. I want you to remember one very important Scripture, man or woman of God, and that is 1 Timothy 4:8 which says, "For bodily exercise profiteth little: but godliness is profitable unto all things, having promise of the life that now is, and of that which is to come."

God says that in verse 8b godliness (living right before God) makes you profitable in all things (blessed in every area of your life). God does not just promise you blessings in heaven only, but He says, "having the promise of the life that now is." In other words there are some promises God has given to you for now that are blessings for living right, and you can experience these promises here on earth. They are found in two Scriptures:

1. Psalm 37:4 which says, "Delight thyself also in the Lord: and he shall give thee the desires of thine heart."
2. Psalm 84:11 which says, "For the Lord God is a sun and shield: the Lord will give grace and glory: no good thing will he withhold from them that walk uprightly."

Then the Lord also promises according to 1Timothy 4:8b promises of that which is to come (in other words in heaven). There is a passage of Scripture for this, which is Mark 10:30 in which God promises many blessings now and eternal life at the end. It reads "But he shall receive an hundredfold now in this time, houses, and brethren, and sisters, and mothers, and children, and lands, with persecutions; and in the world to come eternal life."

God said that He is getting ready to exalt you because you were chosen to fly and not be grounded. You are not a chicken, you are an eagle. You were chosen to fly over your circumstances, and you were destined to succeed. *Failure is not an option*, and I want you to let go of that unneeded baggage today so you can stop being grounded.

6 Single Parenting (How Are You Doing It?)

You single man and woman, how do you do it? You maintain work, school, church, personal concerns, paying all the bills by yourself, trying to reach personal goals, and then trying to raise children. Raising children is a full time job all by itself, let alone when trying to work and go to school as well. While you have been beating yourself up about what you are not doing, let me inform you that there are families with two parents, and they are doing very little in raising their children. So even in your shortcomings repeat this statement after me, "I may not be the best parent, but I'm not done yet."

This chapter is written to give you some biblical examples and principles in raising a child while being single, saved, and somehow surviving in a seductive society. You obviously have a system that may be already working; I want to offer you some things that may just add to it.

The first thing you must do in single parenting is to become organized and a master day planner. You must understand that Satan and society throughout the day try to plant thoughts and wickedness into the mind of your child. You have to strategically organize your day to fit some personal time with you and your children so you can balance out the wrong things they heard and learned with the right things you can deposit in them.

Proverbs 22:15a tell us that "Foolishness is bound in the heart of a child." In your day planner, usually the average 8 to 5 p.m. worker gets up around 5:30 to 6:30 a.m. and gets dressed and gets their children dressed and ready. If you are blessed, you try to have a quick breakfast in between getting dressed and out the door. So when do you have morning time with your child? When you get in the car with your child and leave your home, you have usually an average of five to thirty minutes with them in traveling time to deposit the spiritual nourishment they need. Cut the radio off and do the most important thing you can do with that child— that is to pray and put that child in God's hands. Have your morning prayer with that child and even let them pray. Matthew 21:22 says, "And all things whatsoever ye shall ask in prayer, believing, ye shall receive."

Ask the Lord for these seven things:

1. Watch over your child
2. Give them wisdom to choose good friends
3. Help them always make right decisions
4. Give them the spirit of wisdom, knowledge, and understanding that they may always succeed in all classes.
5. Protect them from all hurt, harm, and danger.

6. Make them the light around others that they may be leaders to Christ and not followers of Satan.
7. Bring them back home safely.

If you pray believing what God said in Matthew 21:22, you will receive it. Usually the other span of time that you have with your child is after school and work. You are in most cases tired while trying to make dinner, going over their homework, getting them ready for bed, sometimes attending church, and trying to wind down yourself.

Remember this statement "You are in control." Say that with me, "I am in control." I need you to take control of your time and your child. What you say goes, and you must put your children on your agenda. First of all you are trying to spend time with them and get all the things done you need to do. Most of your children go somewhere after school for about one and a half to two and a half hours, either to a babysitter, home, or an after school program. Wherever that place is, you need to ensure that your child uses that time to finish all or at least the majority of that homework. This way when you get home, you just have to check to make sure it's done. It may take you giving your child some special perks or just threatening to discipline him if his homework is not done (whatever works!).

Proverbs 23:13–14 tells us, "Withhold not correction from the child: for if thou beatest him with the rod, he shall not die. Thou shalt beat him with the rod, and shalt deliver his soul from hell."

Now your main concern is to spend time with your child

while getting all your items completed. Let's incorporate the two together. First when you get home:

1. Make your child sit at the kitchen table and finish their homework, and while you are cooking, you can assist them with any problems or questions. The key is not to let them go to their room, but stay at the kitchen table. Room time can be later on, but school work is first. This takes care of two things at the same time.
2. If your child finishes their homework before time or before you finish cooking, a good way of pouring into your child godly principles is to have them help you cook while you talk. I learned that my daughters appreciated dinner more when they helped me cook it. While you and the kids are making dinner, (advice: let them do the simple stuff like stirring!) you will find in mixing seasonings and ingredients that God will give you things to say to correlate with your cooking. For example as you are mixing certain ingredients, you can say all ingredients don't mix well together, and so it is in life everyone you may want to be friends with may not mix well with you. Then another example you can teach them is that some ingredients look unappealing, but when you taste them they taste good. Tell them in life just because people are not popular and don't look quote unquote good on the outside, doesn't mean they are not beautiful and have good hearts on the inside. Teach them it's not what's on the outside that makes a good friend, but what is on the inside. Cooking together gives you time

together, and oh yes, don't forget the eating part. Now the dinner table experience needs to happen every night. Even if it's just hot dogs and homemade fries, make it happen.

3. Now after dinner you will have two agenda items to complete, which are personal time and getting things ready for the next day. This would be a good time to give your child free time, which allows you either free time as well or you can trade that time to prepare for tomorrow, then after that you can have the rest of your night to yourself. After the kids' leisure time, send them off to bed. This gives you the rest of the night to yourself, or if you traded earlier then this gives you time to prepare for tomorrow.

Remember keeping control of your kids is the key.

Single man and single woman, I share the concern and even worry many times about my children and their future. As I prepared to write this chapter, the Lord wanted me to tell you "If you do your part, I will make sure to do mine." The Lord said that He already has a plan for your child and your prayers are definitely heard in His ears. The Lord not only hears your prayers but will answer them and take care of your child.

As a single mother, you have to be the mother and the father. As a single father, you have to be the father and the mother. There will come times where you don't feel you can relate to your child in certain instances. They are on one level, and you are on another. They think you are too old to understand what they are facing, when they don't realize you've been their age before and had desires and issues just like they have now. The problem is today most parents try to relate to their kids by trying to be their friends too much, and they lose the foundation of parenthood authority. We try to dress like they do so we can relate to them so they feel comfortable talking to us about sex, relationships, their issues, etc. The main reason why you've tried to develop that type of relationship was so your children would feel comfortable telling you what they are facing. You also hope to get them to talk about it before they experience it. Your hope is to stop them from doing wrong. The problem is that you don't know about it until it's done. We as parents have lost the fear factor system and the spiritual connection with God which always warns us before something happens to our children. It is that connection in your prayer time that amazes your child because you tell them what they are thinking before they can act on it. When we were growing up, the main reason why I did not do the things I wanted to do was because I feared the consequences of my decisions.

So what's your main concern, stopping the child before they do something you don't approve of or being their friend and hearing about it after it's already done. We need parents in this generation, not friends.

Remember what we say about our children is what happens to our children. I don't care what your child's shortcomings and struggles are, don't you speak negative words over your child. You are probably the only one in your child's life who will ever speak life over your child. Everyone else in their life speaks what they won't be, while your mouth speaks what they will be. As soon as Satan can get you so frustrated with your child that you speak negative words over your child, he has won a battle because he knows life and death are in the power of the tongue. If Satan gets you to speak death over your tongue by getting you to speak words like knucklehead, you are just like your daddy or mama; you will never be nothing, etc. You must understand that since that child came out of you or through you, and since you are a child of God, that means there is greatness all up in your child. You as a parent have to find out what are your children's strengths and help them maximize in their strengths. Their weaknesses seem to be the most evident to you, but you have to realize that everyone has weaknesses so stop focusing on their weaknesses so much. You and God are the only ones in their lives who know their strengths and know how to help bring out what's in them. I want you to not handle all their weaknesses at one time because that will frustrate you and them, but find one at a time and if you do not have the ability to help them overcome them then seek help for them in just that one weakness. You are their cheerleader, and remember if you can help them, there may come a day when God uses them to help support you.

Your children need you because the devil and the world are trying to ruin them. Give them to God now and ask Him how to raise the children, and He will direct you. Also remember that God's plan for your children was predetermined before their birth. This is proven in Romans 9:11 when Paul writes about Jacob and Esau and how God had a plan for Jacob to be blessed even before he came in the world and did all those bad things.

Romans 9:11 says, "For the children being not yet born, neither having done any good or evil, that the purpose [plan of God for your child] of God according to election [who God decides to bless] might stand, not of works, but of him that calleth."

Even when they are out there seeming to be out of control, God knows how and when to bring them back in. Ask the prodigal son's daddy.

7 Praising God for What's Not Here Yet

Have you ever praised God for something you hadn't got yet? I just want to prepare you right now for what you been waiting for. I know as a Christian you have heard preachers tell you "The best is yet to come," "Your blessings on the way," "You ain't seen nothing yet," "Your latter shall be greater than your former," and great biblical statements such as that. We all hear these, but they never tell us on how to endure the process while we are waiting. In this chapter I want to show you biblical principles that show us how we praise God before the blessings come.

First of all to praise for where you are going, you have to appreciate where you are. I praise God for what I don't have yet because I understand that the waiting period is preparation time to prepare me to learn how to be thankful, how to keep, and how to appreciate what God is sending my way.

First Thessalonians 5:18 says, "In everything give thanks: for this is the will of God in Christ Jesus concerning you."

God's will is greater than your desire. God is telling you "I dare you to praise me for where you are, because no matter how bad it looks it's preparing you for what's to come."

You sometime don't appreciate the good unless you have at one time experienced the bad. Man of God or woman of God, you must understand that your present season is giving you substance to maintain that which is to come. This preparing I am talking about is what that Apostle Paul was speaking of in Philippians 4:11–13.

In verse eleven he says, "Not that I speak in respect of want." He says not that I need anything, because what I have is indicative of the season I am in. He goes on to say, "for I have learned in whatsoever state I am in, therewith to be content." Paul says, child of God, whatever state, whatever place, whatever stage of your life you're in (lonely, suffering persecution, being without in any area of your life), know that God caused it so that your sufficiency is not in the things or people you have but in your relationship and confidence in the Lord.

In verse twelve Paul lays it on thick by saying, "I know both how to be abased [brought low or been humiliated] and I know how to abound [be prevalent, successful, and live in plenty]."

In life we all have had some good points and some bad points, points of success and points of depression. Paul is teaching us that in life every day won't be sunny, but in cloudy days know that the cloudy days bring about a hunger for the sunny. Your current state keeps you hungry for the blessing to come; it causes you to pray for it, fast for it, cry for it, and shout for it. The plan of God is to draw you closer to Him, so in your press for your blessing it causes you to get closer to God. You being drawn closer to God is not only getting you closer to what is to come, but also is giving you a deeper relationship with God. This is so that when you get your blessing you can't forget God because now the relationship is more important than the blessing.

Man of God and woman of God, I got sick of seeing people who didn't do as much for the Lord as I felt I had yet were more blessed than I was. They hadn't prayed and fasted as much as I had, and hadn't served God as diligently as I felt I had, but yet were walking away with blessings I had been crying to God for. Have you ever said to God, "This is not fair"? I am finding out with God that because I have spent more time with Him, He expects more from me and excellence from me in worship and service.

Child of God, the Lord wants me to tell you that because you are special in His sight, your blessing is sure to come. The only thing we must be cognizant of is that God has given us *steps* to get what is to come, and we must follow them. Until we implement these steps properly and biblically, somebody may have our blessing until we get it right.

All this is found in 2 Samuel 6:1–13. This is the Scripture where David was bringing the Ark of the Covenant (presence of God) back to Jerusalem. We are going to dissect this passage of Scripture and give you principles of how to praise God for what you don't have yet. Principle one is very important; are you ready?

Principle #1—"You can't expect the blessings of God by doing what carnal and worldly people do."

In verse three David attempts to transport the Ark of the

Covenant (presence of God) back to Jerusalem so the Israelites could experience the security and presence of God again. The problem was since they had not transported the Ark for over a century, they were not use to bringing in the presence of God (Ark of the Covenant) properly. Let me stop there for a moment. When you have not praised God for the bad as well as the good for a long time, you really haven't worshipped. Worship is when you adore God for who He is in your life. Just like David, when we haven't did it for a long time, we start following the example of carnal and worldly minded people. These people tell you to be reserved and that it doesn't take all of that, or that you don't have to shout. It's those people who try to get you to stay in a box, but when you really think about what God has brought you out of, saved you from getting into, and what He has planned in store for you, you need to go back to the right way of bringing in the presence of God, which is found in praise and worship.

David did not follow the proper way, but did what the worldly folk did to transport the ark. Over in 1 Samuel chapters five and six, the Philistines conquered Israel and stole the Ark of the Covenant from them. The Philistines made a great mistake because God showed them that His presence is only for the true worshippers. When they placed the Ark next to their god (Dagon) in their temple, the presence of God made their god fall down and worship God. Then the next day God cut off the head and hands of Dagon, and only the tail was left. God was proving to them that His presence and blessings are only for His people. That's good news, child of God, because God is teaching us that even though we see people who have possessions like the Philistines of things that seem like the glory of God, they won't stay with them for long. (Also, don't forget that Israel lost the presence of God because of their sin.) First Samuel 5:11 said that because God didn't belong there, deadly destruction broke out in the city of the Philistines. Death and disease broke out to prove you can't keep what belongs to the child of God. What God has for you is only for you. He just wants you to bring Him back to your house the right way first; then the blessings will come with His presence. In 1 Samuel 6:7, the Philistines made a cart and had it connected to two oxen to pull it. Also to get the wrath of God off of them, they sent it back with an offering of jewels of gold. On the cart they laid the Ark of the Covenant and transported it back to Israel. Now the question is why God let them get away with putting the Ark on a cart and not transporting it the proper way. First of all the only ones who were ordained to carry the Ark of the Covenant were Levite priests, which in Philistia there were none, and second of all, they had no knowledge on how to transport it because they were not God's people. So God spared them for not having the right people and not having access to the knowledge of how to carry His presence. For this same reason, worldly people are walking around with your stuff, and it seems like they are getting away with it. First of all Hebrews 12:6 says, "For whom the Lord loveth he chasteneth" (gives a whooping when they're wrong). Then over in verse eight it says, "But if God does not chastise you, then you are a bastard and not a son." If God does not whoop people who do wrong and they still prosper in sin, that means they are not His kids. They may seem blessed now, but their end will be destruction and hell's fire. Only what you do for Christ will last. So in 2 Samuel 6:3 instead of David doing his homework and finding out the right way to bring the Ark of the Covenant (the presence of God, the blessings of God, and the security of God) he followed the ways of the worldly Philistines. In 2 Samuel 6:3 he put the Ark on a new cart and connected the cart with oxen to pull it to Jerusalem. Child of God, the Lord wants you to understand the worldly way is to praise God for what you have only, but God's way is to praise Him in advance. In verse five David and the people are going through the formality of praise but have the wrong concept of bringing the presence into the city. You can praise with sound, but if you don't do it God's way, it won't yield you the blessings you expect to receive in praise. In 2 Samuel 6:6 David and the people arrive at Nachon's threshing floor, and as the oxen walk on the threshing floor, they cause the cart to tip over. This occurred at Nachon's threshing floor because the threshing floor was a symbol of separating the wheat (holiness) from the tare (corruption and evilness). In Jewish times when the farmers brought the sheaves of wheat from the fields, they would lay them on the threshing floor, and they would have the two oxen with yokes around their necks with a rope tied to the yoke and extended to a great stone in the middle of the threshing floor. This would cause the oxen to circle around the floor and stump out the sheaves thereby separating the wheat from the chaff. So the threshing floor was the place where God is speaking symbolically to David, the people, and us that when you are invoking His presence into your life improperly He will cause a shaking to occur in your life to separate the bad way from the good way.

The threshing floor was God saying, "David, I have told you all how to bring the Ark (God's presence, God's blessings, and God's security) into the city, and since you are using the Philistine's way (worldly way) instead of my way, I am going to shake things up to make you stop and give up the worldly way and do it my way saith the Lord.

Child of God, one of the reasons we have not yet got from God what we are asking for is because God is saying to us you are not provoking my presence the right way. God says, I want you to praise me in advance, and you are waiting on the blessing before you praise me. God said "I told you that when I come and bring my presence (security, blessings, and me) you must want it and then follow my precepts and examples and praise me before you get me." In 2 Samuel 6:7–9 God deals with a man named Uzzah who tries to stop the Ark from falling when the oxen start shaking it. Uzzah was probably just trying to be helpful, but God said when the Philistines were dealing with me I overlooked it because they knew no better. David and Uzzah, you are expected to know that handling me any kind of way is not going to work. So God struck down Uzzah for touching the Ark because only consecrated Levites were suppose to touch it, and Uzzah was not one. One thing I want to capture is Uzzah was not just any Joe Blow off the street. Uzzah was the son of Abinadab who was the one whose house the Ark of the Covenant was at between the time of the Philistines dropping it off and David coming to get it. Uzzah and his family had been in the presence of the Ark for almost a century (one hundred years). I believe that Uzzah probably felt that since he had been in the place where the presence of God was for a long time, that gave him the right to do what he wanted to and it would still help bring the presence of God to the city.

Children of God, in the church we have people with the same mentality. Just because I have been in the church (place of God) for many years, I think I can do what I want to do and worship how I want to worship. In most churches the presence of God is absent because we want to praise and worship how we want to and not how God said to do. If you want results, praise and worship until the glory of God comes down. Get rid of tradition and time limits; you need the presence of God, and we need to tarry until He comes.

Principle #2—"God will let you see others blessed in order to drive you to seek His face."

In 2 Samuel 6:10–12 David decides to take the Ark of the Covenant to the house of Obed-edom to keep while David plans how to get the Ark of the Covenant to his house. The text says in 2 Samuel 6:11 that the Ark of the Covenant stayed at Obed-edom's house for three months, and while it was there Obed-edom and all his family got blessed like crazy from the Lord. Verse twelve said that when David heard of this he made provision to get it to his house.

It took God blessing Obed-edom's house to drive David to seek the proper way of moving the Ark (God's presence, God's blessings, and God's security) to his house. The reason why God will let you see others in the church blessed more than you is to drive you to seek the proper way to get God's presence into your life.

The same story is found in 1 Chronicles, and it gives more

details on how he moved the ark into the city. First Chronicles 15:1–2 said David checked the history and found out that no one was suppose to carry the Ark of God except the Levite priests according to Deuteronomy 10:8. As we flip back to 2 Samuel 6:13, we see that David is so excited that now the Ark is coming into the city and house. He knows that when God shows up He brings His presence, His blessings, and His security with Him. David gets so caught up in what is about to happen or to come that he forget who he is (the king) and who is around and dances with all his might so much that he dances out of his clothes according to 2 Samuel 6:20b.

I'm writing this to inform and encourage you, don't wait until the battle is over—*shout now*! Psalm 71:14 says, "But I will hope continually, and will yet praise thee more and more." The writer says I'm gonna have faith until it happens but still praise Him more each day. When you find out how to move God according to His Word, and how He wants you to thank Him in advance, your blessing will be on the way.

(*Just for a moment praise God for what is coming your way.*)

You have to be like Abraham and have confidence in God. Romans 4:20–21 said, "He staggered not at the promise of God through unbelief; but was strong in faith, giving glory to God; And being fully persuaded that, what he had promised, he was able also to perform."

You need to praise God before your blessing comes because you know that if God promises, He has to bring it to past. Stop staggering, stop letting doubt hold you up from praising because verse twenty said Abraham was strong in faith giving glory to God. This meant his faith said "I know God will bring it to past," and he glorified God even before the miracle happened. Verse twenty-one says, "And being fully persuaded (completely convinced) that what He had promised, He was able also to perform."

Are you convinced? Hasn't God already proved to you He has His hand upon you? That's why you have shelter, food on your table, clothes on your back, dreams, and some dreams that have already come true. You need to be convinced that what God promised He's able to perform. If He told you it's yours, shout now because you have a promise from the Man who writes the check, touches the heart, and prepares the victory.

8 I Need Security and Safety

Life can throw some devastating punches. In life we all have put our trust and hopes in people at one time or another. We've trusted that Mama or Daddy would stay around; we trusted that girlfriend, boyfriend, husband, or wife would never betray us. We trusted that job would be the place we'd retire at; we trusted that family member or family friend to never rape or molest us; and we trusted that friend would have never turned on or backstabbed us. Through all the needed security we relied upon and hoped in, we found out brothers and sisters somehow and someway always let us down. I keep saying to myself I need security. I need someone to make me feel secure in my image, my self-worth and give me security in how I look, security in feeling wanted or loved, security in my finances, etc.

I need that someone who helps me tie up the loose ends of my life that if they are left untied my whole life would unravel. Brothers and sisters, I want you to know that true security can only be found in God, because all the people and things we have chosen to be our security are always subject to change. God said in Malachi 3:6, "For I am the Lord, I change not." When everyone else gets fickle on me, God says, if you seek your security in me I will never change on you, I will never act like I love you one day and then act like I am not sure the next. God said, I will never act like you have security and longevity with me then in a few months tell you I don't think it's gonna work out.

God wants you to feel so secure in Him that He says in Malachi 3:5, "I'm gonna judge and be a swift witness [swift destruction] against:

1. Sorcerers—Folk that tried to curse you
2. Adulterers—Folk that slept around on you
3. False swearers—Folk who lied to you and broke commitments with you.
4. Oppressors at the places where you earn wages—Folk that treated you badly on your job and didn't want to pay you right.
5. Oppressors of the widow—God's gonna help the widows and protect them against the folk who'll try to take from or hurt them.
6. Oppressors of the fatherless—God's gonna judge that fathers and mothers that left you high and dry and deal with folk who took advantage of you because you had no covering of a father.
7. Oppressors of the stranger—God's gonna get the people who took advantage of you when you were in need and made you do things you didn't want to do to give you what you needed.

Now that's what I call security!

The word *security* is defined as:

1. Protection from or defense from any kind of danger.
2. Sense of feeling wanted or loved.
3. Sense of not feeling alone and having stability financially

Many times single women desire security because they fear walking home late at night when no one is looking out for them. There's the desire of wanting security as when you go places you have that man who will not let anyone say or do something to you. The man is a security blanket that makes you feel safe.

For men we need women to make us feel secure in who we are in most cases. Having a woman on his arm makes a man feel like he's complete in most cases. When a man has beauty on his arm, he walks around like he has conquered the world, and his self confidence skyrockets. Without a man if you are a woman and without a woman if you are a man, you develop a sense of fear or a lack of confidence.

I want to encourage you that God will not leave you alone. Let me say that again, "God will not leave you alone."

Second Timothy 1:8 encourages, "For God hath not given us the spirit of fear, but of power, love, and a sound mind." God says, man of God and woman of God, I want you to have a sound mind (a mind that is focused and not afraid to take chances, confident in one's self, and finally secure in who you are). Thirdly, I want you to have love. God is saying to us that we can't be afraid to love again even after we have been hurt. First John 4:18 says "There is no fear in love; but perfect love casteth out fear: because fear hath torment. He that feareth is not made perfect in love."

One thing we must not do is to make the next one pay for the mistakes of the last one. Now being cautious and extra careful is one thing, but treating the new person God sends us in our lives badly because of what the last one did is wrong. Third, God has given us power. The word *power* in the Greek means a miracle, a supernatural ability, an abundance, strength, and mighty works. God said, man and woman of God, your security and safety has to be in me who provides you with supernatural ability, an abundance of things you need, strength in times and places where you feel vulnerable, and the ability to perform mighty works which allows you to have the edge over the next person.

Again, security and safety means protection from danger. Being single often means you have no one watching your back or keeping an eye out for you in case of danger. I want you to have confidence from this day on that you have the greatest protector watching over you.

In Psalm 71:7 the writer says, "I am as a wonder unto many; but thou art my strong refuge." The writer says, woman and man of God, people wonder how you are making it alone, and how it is you can walk home alone and not fear, and how you can feel protected when no one is visibly there. The Lord wanted me to remind you that He is our strong refuge, our place of strong security, and our keeper from hurt, harm, and danger. Psalms 18:3–9, 17–19 really encourages us by saying,

> I will call upon the Lord, Who is to be praised; so

> shall I be saved from my enemies. 4. The cords or bands of death surrounded me, and the streams of ungodliness and torrents of ruin terrified me. 5. The cords of Sheol [the place of the dead] surrounded me; the snares of death confronted and came upon me. 6. In my distress [when seemingly closed in] I called upon the Lord, and cried to my God; He heard my voice out of His temple [heavenly dwelling place], and my cry came before Him, to His very ears. 7. Then the earth quaked and rocked; the foundations also of the mountains trembled, they moved and were shaken, because He was indignant and angry. 8. There went up smoke from His nostrils, and lightning out of His mouth devoured; coals were kindled by it. 9. He bowed the heavens also, and came down; and thick darkness was under His feet. 17. He delivered me from my strong enemy, and from those who hated and abhorred me; for they were too strong for me. 18. They confronted and came upon me I the day of my calamity; but the Lord was my stay and support. 19. He brought me forth also into a large place; He was delivering me, because He was pleased with me and delighted in me.
>
> (AMP)

Safety and security also is the sense of feeling wanted and loved. I don't care who you are and what you say, everyone wants to be loved. As a young man you always wanted the approval of your father or father figure. On the inside you wanted him to say, "Son, I'm proud of you" or "I love you." Every young girl wants to hear their daddy call them a princess (without an underlining meaning of sex) and make them feel beautiful. That father or father figure's words help shape the confidence and self-image of that young girl.

In all of this there is a psychological aspect that is misunderstood, and that is when someone either has not received this or is used to receiving this, they either crave the attention due to always receiving it or because they never received it. This sense of needing security in love is what gets singles in trouble in relationships. We begin to look at the person we just started dating one day ago and expect them to fill the void all the way from childhood. This causes us to make bad decisions on giving up sex to get the love we always wanted. It causes us to try to buy their love by buying them clothes, jewelry, and even houses and cars, depending on how bad it is. The sense of needing love causes us to fall into deep depression (especially when we see someone else getting it: like married folk, friends, and even kissy strangers).

I want to encourage you about security in oneself. First of all if nobody ever showed you love or made you feel good about yourself, stop whining right now. You have to love yourself first! Go over to a mirror for a second. Yes, I said to a mirror; go on now. Look at yourself and smile, and repeat this after me. "Hey there, my name is (state you name) and not only am I a child of God, but despite anybody's opinion, I got it goin' on! (Repeat it two more times for the Father, Son, and Holy Ghost.)

You got it goin' on. One reason why God allowed others not to give you the sense of security you needed was because God wanted you to have the need fulfilled by Him and Him first. He wanted you to know that the Creator of all men and women, those you wanted to feel loved by and those you wanted to just hear words of encouragement from, all were made by Him. They are nothing but small representatives of the Big and Real One. He wants you to know your Daddy in heaven is proud of you and loves you. Let Him be your true security first, and then once others come in your life and maybe don't fulfill their vow to always be there for you, you already will have that hole in your heart filled, and it won't hurt you as much.

Once you receive true love then you will know how to discern counterfeit. You can't trick me with a Shasta Cola because I know what Coca Cola is supposed to taste like. Shasta Cola is a watered down version, and that does not satisfy me—I want the real thing.

God's Love toward you is immeasurable. Why can't we learn to love Him as He loves us? Psalms 63:1–9 says,

> O God, thou art my God; early will I seek thee: my soul thirsteth for thee, my flesh longeth for thee in a dry and thirsty land, where no water is; 2. To see thy power and thy glory, so as I have seen thee in the sanctuary. 3. Because thy loving-kindness is better than life, my lips shall praise thee. 4. Thus will I bless thee while I live: I will lift up my hands in thy name. 5. My soul shall be satisfied as with marrow and fatness; and my mouth shall praise thee with joyful lips: 6. When I remember thee upon my bed, and meditate on thee in the night watches. 7. Because thou hast been my help, therefore in the shadow of thy wings will I rejoice. 8. My soul followeth hard after thee: thy right hand upholdeth me. 9. But those that seek my soul, to destroy it, shall go into the lower parts of the earth.

The psalmist gives us seven major love handles to focus on:

1. I love God so much I get up early just to feel His Presence. (Verse one)
2. I crave His presence. Without Him I feel like a person in the desert with no water. (Verse one)
3. I want to feel God outside the church like I feel Him inside the church (verse two)
4. God, your love for me is better than life itself. I want God's love first because He loves me unconditionally. So my lips will praise you, oh Lord. Instead of always talking about what somebody did for you, talk about what the Lord has done for you. (Verses three through five)
5. Even while in bed, I am thinking about how you did not let my enemies shame me. How you kept me safe, blessed me, and kept my sanity in insane times. Oh God, you are so wonderful. (Verse six)
6. You were my hiding place when life tried to find me and destroy me. I hid under the shadow of your wings. (Verse seven)
7. As I sought after you, oh God, you kept me lifted up above my enemies with your right hand. He still has a left hand that smacks the devil out of your way. (Verse eight)

There are other love notes that God wrote you. Won't you take a moment to read them:

1. Psalms 103:1–5

Bless the Lord, O my soul: and all that is within me,

bless his holy name. 2. Bless the Lord, O my soul, and forget not all his benefits: 3. Who forgiveth all thine iniquities; who healeth all thy diseases; 4. Who redeemeth thy life from destruction; who crowneth thee with loving-kindness and tender mercies; 5. Who satisfieth thy mouth with good things; so that thy youth is renewed like the eagles.

2. Deuteronomy 7:7

The Lord did not set his love upon you, nor choose you, because ye were more in number than any people; for ye were the fewest of all people. God said I loved you before you became all of that. I loved you when no one else did. Not for what you could do for me, but for what I wanted to do for you.

3. Romans 5:8

But God commendeth his love toward us, in that, while we were yet sinners, Christ died for us.

4. Romans 8:38–39

For I am persuaded, that neither death, nor life, nor angels, nor principalities, nor powers, nor things present, nor things to come, Nor height, nor depth, nor any other creature, shall be able to separate us from the love of God, which is in Christ Jesus our Lord.

5. 1 John 4:9–10

In this was manifested the love of God toward us, because that God sent his only begotten Son into the world, that we might live through him. Herein is

> love, not that we loved God, but that he loved us, and sent his Son to be the propitiation for our sins.

6. 1 John 3:16

> Hereby perceive we the love of God, because he laid down his life for us: and we ought to lay down our lives for the brethren.

Security is also having the confidence of having another source of income. If you were previously married or in a relationship where you had a supplemental income through a spouse or significant other, you know what I am saying. We many times look for relationships to help us meet our financial obligations. That other person brings you security by paying your bills. Many times as singles, we sacrifice our holiness by sleeping around with that person to get them to help with paying our bills. When are you going to wake up and realize that God is Jehovah Jireh—God my Provider? One of the reasons why we have relied on others to give us financial security is because since we decided to do right by God and live right, we really have not tried God on His Word to meet our every needs.

Let's read Matthew 6:25–34 which says,

> Therefore I say unto you, Take no thought for your life, what ye shall eat, or what ye shall drink; nor yet for your body, what ye shall put on. Is not the life more than meat, and the body than raiment? 26. Behold the fowls of the air: for they sow not, neither do they reap, nor gather into barns; yet your heavenly Father feedeth them. Are ye not much better than they? 27. Which

> of you by taking thought can add one cubit unto his stature? 28. And why take ye thought for raiment? Consider the lilies of the field, how they grow; they toil not, neither do they spin: 29. And yet I say unto you, that even Solomon in all his glory was not arrayed like one of these. 30. Wherefore, if God so clothe the grass of the field, which to day is, and to morrow is cast into the oven, shall he not much more clothe you, O ye of little faith? 31. Therefore take no thought, saying, What shall we eat? Or, what shall we drink? Or, Wherewithal shall we be clothed? 32. (For after all these things do the Gentiles seek:) for your heavenly Father knoweth that ye have need of all these things. 33. But seek ye first the kingdom of God, and his righteousness; and all these things shall be added unto you. 34. Take therefore no thought for the morrow: for the morrow shall take thought for the things of itself. Sufficient unto the day is the evil thereof.

In this passage of Scripture, Matthew is encouraging us that we have a heavenly Father who is concerned about us, and if we can put our trust in Him, He will never let us down. Then just one chapter over Matthew teaches us in Matthew 7:7–11 by saying:

> Ask and it shall be given you; seek, and ye shall find; knock, and it shall be opened unto you: 8. For every one that asketh receiveth; and he that seeketh findeth; and to him that knocketh it shall be opened. 9. Or what man is there of you, whom if his son ask bread, will he give him a stone? 10. Or if he ask a fish, will he give him a serpent? 11. If ye then, being evil,

> know how to give good gifts unto your children, how much more shall your Father which is in heaven give good things to them that ask him?

I don't know about you, but I am tired of feeling like I have to owe somebody to just survive. You don't want to have to sacrifice your mental health, body, and soul just to get your bills paid and get nice things. I'd rather trust God and be satisfied with what the Lord has given me than sacrifice my integrity with God by pleasing them sinfully to get what I need.

God told me to tell you that what He has given you is what He wants you to have and if you hold out and be faithful the best is not just yet to come, but that you are on the brink of financial breakthrough. The first lesson is for us to be thankful for what He has already provided.

You do not have to covet or envy what others have. God has things in store for you. Just read Hebrews 13:5 which says "Let your conversation be without covetousness; and be content with such things as ye have: for he hath said, I will never leave thee, nor forsake thee."

God said, I ain't going anywhere. I am your financial security, saith the Lord. Paul the Apostle tells us how to trust God as the provision. In Philippians 4:11–13 Paul says,

> Not that I speak in respect of want: for I have learned, in whatsoever state I am, therewith to be content. 12. I know both how to be abased, and I know how to abound: every where and in all things I am instructed both to be full and to be hungry, both to abound and to suffer need. 13. I can do all things through Christ which strengtheneth me.

Paul says I have learned that whatever state I am in God willed it and if God said it I don't have to worry about it. He says I will not let my predicament dictate my reaction or outlook or perspective on the situation. In other words I will keep my joy despite whatever happens. In verse twelve, Paul tells us he has been humbled or brought down by life's shifts, and then life has been good. He then goes on to say every place he is in and everything about his life is all according to God, and He will allow me to be full or hungry, to be blessed materialistically and then to suffer need. In all of this Paul says in verse thirteen I still can do all things that are in my heart to do because Christ will strengthen me.

God told me to tell you, man or woman of God, that you are secure in Him, not in a man or woman. He also said for you to be thankful for what and where you are *first*. One of the reasons we have not got the latter rain is because we have not thanked Him for the former rain. Read 1 Timothy 6:6–10 which says,

> But godliness with contentment is great gain. 7. For we brought nothing into this world, and it is certain we can carry nothing out. 8. And having food and raiment let us be therewith content. 9. But they that will be rich fall into temptation and a snare, and into many foolish and hurtful lusts, which drown men in destruction and perdition. 10. For the love of money is the root of all evil: which while some coveted after, they have erred from the faith, and pierced themselves through with many sorrows.

God told me to tell you that a person with a true relationship with God that has his needs met is much more well off than a person with riches who doesn't have a true relationship with God. When God is calling for the true relationship with Him, He will allow you (the pursued) to suffer hardship so you will become (the pursuer) in seeking God.

Living holy for the Lord according to 1 Timothy 6:6 is a greater gain than living in sin. I am not saying that God wants you barely making it or broke, but I am saying He promised you if you walk upright before Him no good thing will He withhold from you as He says in Psalm 84:11b.

Read Psalm 37:16 which says, "A little that a righteous man hath is better than the riches of many wicked."

Stop sleeping around and living unholy just to get the bills paid, clothes bought, and your other needs met. Where is your commitment to God? Don't you trust Him, and isn't He worth waiting on? Read Psalms 34:9–10 where David encourages us by saying, "O fear the Lord, ye his saints: for there is no want to them that fear him.

The young lions do lack, and suffer hunger: but they that seek the Lord shall not want any good thing."

Walk in victory, child of God, even in things you don't always understand or those you can't control. Child of God, Proverbs 3:5–6 says, "Trust in the Lord with all thine heart; and lean not unto thine own understanding. In all thy ways acknowledge him and he shall direct thy paths." Sometime you feel like God has forsaken you, but David said in Psalm 31:22 "For I said in my haste [in worrying and before really thinking], I am cut off from before thine eyes [I don't have God with me and helping me]: nevertheless thou hearest the voice of my supplications when I cried unto thee." So now since God hears you, but is proving you as verse twenty-three says, "O love the Lord, all ye His saints; for the Lord preserves the faithful, and plentifully rewardeth the proud doer."

9 What Stopped Me from Getting That Special Someone?

You are probably saying, pastor, I have been in relationships with people that I just knew they were the right person for me. It seemed like just before we got to the next level, either they went sideways on me, or I find out a serious relationship breaking secret, or they wanted to for whatever reason to call it off, or I just suddenly lost interest in them. Pastor, why did this happen to me out of all people; don't I deserve that special someone in my life?

Child of God, your heavenly Father knows what is coming ahead in the future. So many times in relationships, we get so emotionally involved that we become blind to the obvious red flags God is showing us to let us know this is gonna cause us headaches in the future. God causes the break up to save you from some heartbreaking truths that He did not want you to go through. So what you thought was God cursing you was actually God saving you.

Many times in looking for Mr. or Ms. Right, we make decisions on relationships based on the visible features and characteristics of a man and of a woman, but God knows what's going on inside of that person's heart. Read Jeremiah 17:9–10 which says, "The heart is deceitful above all things, and desperately wicked: who can know it? I the Lord search the heart; I try the reins, even to give every man according to his ways, and according to the fruit of his doings."

Like I said to you before, marriage is not just all about sex and companionship; *marriage is a ministry*. God puts two people together who He feels He can trust to minister to the issues, hurt, or weaknesses of the heart of each person. So many times we don't know the deep-rooted issues within that partner we are involved with, but since God does, He knows if you can handle the storms this person is going to go through in the process of their deliverance from those issues. Some issues are molestation and rape (these cause issues of not trusting and not liking touches), physical abuse, missing parents (who never taught how to treat a man or woman), lacking natural affection (no idea how to love and never was shown love), mental abuse, drugs, alcoholic problems, etc. So when God didn't let a past relationship happen it was Him telling you either that the person you were with may have been too much for you to handle while you are trying to fulfill all the desires of your heart. Yes, I know you are saying right now, "I could have handled it," but we all have a tendency of signing up for a job wholeheartedly and committing to it until the job gets to be too much and then we want to jump ship. Child of God, God wants you to know marriage is a lifetime commitment.

God knows what He has for you, and God's gift for you is always good. Read James 1:17 which says, "Every good gift and every perfect gift is from above, and cometh down from the Father of lights, with whom is no variableness, neither shadow of turning."

God says, child of God, I want to give you someone who will not only minister to your physical needs, but also to those deep inner hurts you've been through. So I want to make sure you are ready for them so you don't scare the one I send away and that they are ready for you so they don't scare you off. Also James 1:17b says that God has "no variableness, neither shadow of turning." This means that once God sends you someone right, there is no wondering if it's going to work. If God sends you your gift of a man or woman, they will be right.

Jeremiah 29:11 tells us, "For I know the thoughts that I think toward you, saith the Lord, thoughts of peace, and not of evil, to give you an expected end." God said I only am thinking thoughts of peace for you (not turmoil or stress because of the wrong person), to give you an expected end or an end of expectation. God said man or woman of God; I want you to have an *expectancy of me sending you a miracle*.

Are you ready and are you expecting God to show up?

Do you know what else really stopped you from getting Mr. or Ms. Right? I call it "the counterfeit." The counterfeit is the person that the devil always sends you before Mr. or Ms. Right shows up. The purpose of the counterfeit is that they actually come to connect to you and drop off their baggage of spirits of heaviness, sin, and many times fornication. Then that means that you are no longer ready for that perfect gift God has prepared for you. Now since you have picked up some unneeded baggage, God has to send you like Israel through the wilderness to experience it all over again; to purge off of you that baggage you just picked up which depending on how often you get into His presence to be refined like that gold. Now you lose one year plus in preparation to again remove bad stuff you picked up. The devil knows that the Word of God says "The Father seeketh such to worship him." In other words God is looking to overtake the people whom He finds that worship Him with blessings. Worshipping God means that I don't ask God for anything; all I tell Him is how much I love Him.

So Satan knows that when you are into God, that you are on the brink of getting from God what He promised you. This means the devil knows that God said in Numbers 23:19, "God is not a man, that he should lie; neither the son of man, that he should repent: hath he said, and shall he not do it? or hath he spoken, and shall he not make it good?" God promised us in Psalm 37:4, "Delight thyself also in the LORD: and he shall give thee the desires of thine heart." So the devil knows that you've been giving God all you got in serving Him, worshipping Him, living for Him, and now he knows God has to do what He said He would do. Now if your desire was for a man or woman, Satan knows the only way you will miss the man or woman God is sending you is if he sends you a counterfeit one to get you focused off the one the Lord is sending.

Who is the counterfeit? Well he or she looks like a Christian, talks like a Christian, walks like a Christian, but when you try to cash them in they have no value. Just like a counterfeit dollar bill, this person looks like a dollar, but the only way you will find out if this person is, is when you try to cash one in and then the teller or cashier will tell you this "money" has no value because it's a counterfeit.

The purpose of the counterfeits is to get you thinking you have something special, when all they are is someone with no value and nothing you can cash in. So right when you have reached a new level in God and suddenly a man or woman shows up, before you say this is my godsend because of how I have been with God, take a moment and make sure he or she is not the counterfeit.

A counterfeit many times comes to you at your most vulnerable state. Right after your heart has been broken either by death of a spouse, divorce, break up, job loss, or feeling unwanted or unattractive. Read Judges 15:1–3 as an example of how a man's heart got broken. It reads,

> But it came to pass within a while after, in the time of wheat harvest, that Samson visited his wife with a kid; and he said, I will go in to my wife into the chamber. But her father would not suffer him to go in. 2. And her father said, I verily thought that thou hadst utterly hated her; therefore I gave her to thy companion: is not her younger sister fairer than she? Take her; I pray thee, instead of her. 3. And Samson said concerning them, now shall I be more blameless than the Philistines, though I do them displeasure.

Samson had been away from his wife for a period of time working, and when he returned he found that his father-in-law had given her away to another man. This obviously broke Samson's heart, and now his pain leaves an open door for a counterfeit to show up and rob him.

The counterfeit shows up in Judges 16:4–21. It reads,

> And it came to pass afterward, that he loved a woman in the valley of Sorek, whose name was Delilah.5. And the lords of the Philistines came up unto her, and said unto her, Entice him, and see wherein his great strength lieth, and by what means we may prevail against him, that we may bind him to afflict him; and we will give thee every one of us eleven hundred pieces of silver. 6. And Delilah said to Samson, Tell me, I pray thee, wherein thy great strength lieth, and wherewith thou mightest be bound to afflict thee. 7. And Samson said unto her, If they bind me with seven green withs that were never dried, then shall I be weak, and be as another man. 8. Then the lords of the Philistines brought up to her seven green withs which had not been dried, and she bound him with them. 9. Now there were men lying in wait, abiding with her in the chamber. And she said unto him, The Philistines be upon thee, Samson. And he breaks the withs, as a thread of tow is broken when it toucheth the fire. So his strength was not known. 10. And Delilah said unto Samson, Behold, thou hast mocked me, and told me lies: now tell me, I pray thee, wherewith thou mightest be bound. 11. And he said unto her, If they bind me fast with new ropes that never were occupied, then shall I be weak, and be as another man. 12. Delilah therefore took new ropes, and bound him therewith, and said unto him, The Philistines be upon thee, Samson.

And there were liers in wait abiding in the chamber. And he breaks them from off his arms like a thread. 13. And Delilah said unto Samson, Hitherto thou hast mocked me, and told me lies: tell me wherewith thou mightest be bound. And he said unto her, if thou weavest the seven locks of my head with the web. 14. And she fastened it with the pin, and said unto him, The Philistines be upon thee, Samson. And he awaked out of his sleep, and went away with the pin of the beam, and with the web. 15. And she said unto him, how canst thou say, I love thee, when thine heart is not with me? Thou hast mocked me these three times, and hast not told me wherein thy great strength lieth. 16. And it came to pass, when she pressed him daily with her words, and urged him, so that his soul was vexed unto death; 17. That he told her all his heart, and said unto her, There hath not come a razor upon mine head; for I have been a Nazarene unto God from my mother's womb: if I be shaven, then my strength will go from me, and I shall become weak, and be like any other man. 18. And when Delilah saw that he had told her all his heart, she sent and called for the lords of the Philistines, saying, come up this once, for he hath shewed me all his heart. Then the lords of the Philistines came up unto her, and brought money in their hand. 19. And she made him sleep upon her knees; and she called for a man, and she caused him to shave off the seven locks of his head; and she began to afflict him, and his strength went from him. 20. And she said, The Philistines be upon thee, Samson. And he awoke out of his sleep, and said, I will go out as at other times before, and shake myself. And he wist not that the

> Lord was departed from him. 21. But the Philistines took him, and put out his eyes, and brought him down to Gaza, and bound him with fetters of brass; and he did grind in the prison house.

This counterfeit Delilah shows up in Samson's life at a point when his heart is broken. She is sent by the enemy because God will never send you anyone who will rob you of your anointing. This counterfeit wins him over with beauty and by telling him what he wanted to hear, the only problem is a counterfeit always wants to know your weaknesses so they can use them for their benefit. They always say the right things because before they make their move they probe you for information on why you are hurt. You began to share with them what you either miss or did not receive. They then start telling you that if they were your man or woman they would fulfill all the things you missed or never received. You think you then have your soul mate when all that person is, is an informed counterfeit. Jesus said in Matthew 12:33c, "For a tree is known by his [or her] fruit." Sometimes you have to wait to see what fruit shows up, to tell what type of tree you have. So in saying that, before you jump into any relationship, sit back and watch that person and wait to see if you have a good tree (person) or corrupt tree (person).

John 10:10a says, "The thief cometh not, but for to steal, and to kill, and to destroy." Satan's purpose of sending the counterfeit to you is to get you caught up and then miss out your blessing up ahead. They are sent to trip you up with sin such as: fornication, adultery, lust, lasciviousness, or covetousness; then that devil accuses you before God saying that you don't deserve the blessing because of what you did. Revelation 12:10c proves it in saying, "for the accuser of our brethren is cast down, which accused them before our God day and night." The devil's accusing thereby causes your blessing to be put on hold. Every time you are about to get blessed or favor, expect the counterfeit.

The counterfeit is here to rob you of your strength as Delilah always asked Samson, "where is your strength?" The way to determine if a person is a counterfeit or not is to see if they try to get you to do anything that would make you lose spiritual strength. I don't care how much they support you and say they love you, if they seduce you to sin; they are counterfeits and eventually will rob you of what you would have received from God.

Where Do I find Mr. or Ms. Right?

I know you are asking, pastor, okay, so where do I find Mr. or Ms. Right? Should I find them at the church, social gatherings, the club, on the internet, through a dating service, a blind date, etc? Let's just be real about this. Do you want to know how to get a man or woman, or do you want to know how to get a husband or wife? The key also is do you want me to tell you what you want to hear or do you want me to tell you what will truly work? You can try it the world's way or God's way. Your friends want you to keep clubbing, but read to them 1 Peter 4:4 which says, "Wherein they think it strange that ye run not with them to the same excess of riot [going out clubbing and drinking all night], speaking evil of you." Tell them you'll try it God's way this time.

If you follow these steps, you will truly find the husband or wife that the Lord has for you. *Are you ready?*

First, to the woman of God, if you follow these steps you won't just get a man, but you will receive "The Man."

1. Stop looking right now!

Wait, pastor, that sounds crazy; what do you mean stop looking now? First of all God cannot go against His Word, but if you follow His Word He can't help but to give you what His Word says.

Proverbs 18:22 says, "Whoso findeth a wife findeth a good thing, and obtaineth favour of the Lord." The Scripture did not say for the woman to find a man, but that the man would find you. The Scripture also did not say a man that finds a woman, but that he finds a wife. There are a lot of women in the world, but there are very few wives. So the first step is to stop looking and then prepare yourself for the next step.

2. Focus all your Attention on serving God and His people.

You cannot truly focus on any one thing if you are looking or thinking on more than one thing. Now if you want success, stop thinking about finding a husband. Now somebody is saying, I have done this already, but I want you to be honest with yourself. Did you really focus on serving and not even consider or think about trying to find a man? Now once you are focused, what is the one thing you must focus on? Read 1 Corinthians 7:34 which says,

> There is difference also between a wife and a virgin. The unmarried woman careth for the things of the Lord, that she may be holy both in body and in spirit: but she that is married careth for the things of the world, how she may please her husband.

You are unmarried so you can care for the things of the Lord. Well, pastor, what does God care for? Read Matthew 25:31–40 which says,

> When the Son of man shall come in his glory, and all the holy angels with him, then shall he sit upon the throne of his glory: 32. And before him shall be gathered all nations: and he shall separate them one from another, as a shepherd divideth his sheep from the goats: 33. And he shall set the sheep on his right hand, but the goats on the left. 34. Then shall the King say unto them on his right hand, Come, ye blessed of my Father, inherit the kingdom prepared for you from the foundation of the world: 35. For I was an hungred, and ye gave me meat: I was thirsty, and ye gave me drink: I was a stranger, and ye took me in: 36. Naked and ye clothed me: I was sick, and ye visited me: I was in prison, and ye came unto me. 37. Then shall the righteous answer him, saying, Lord, when saw we thee an hungred, and fed thee? or thirsty, and gave thee drink? 38. When saw we thee a stranger, and took thee in? or naked, and clothed thee? 39. Or when saw we thee sick, or in prison, and came unto thee? 40. And the King shall answer and say unto them, Verily I say unto you, Inasmuch as ye have done it unto one of the least of these my brethren, ye have done it unto me.

God cares for people who have a need. Now when you can serve the ones that God cares for, your blessing is right around the corner.

(Repeat this after me) "*God, don't forget.*"

This is exemplified in Hebrews 6:10 when God promises saying, "For God is not unrighteous to forget your work and labour of love, which ye have shewed toward his name, in that ye have ministered to the saints, and do minister." Child of God, the Lord will not forget to bless the ones who bless His saints. God blesses women who don't do good to people to get a man, but do good to people to please God. Just so you believe this step let me give you two examples of women in the Bible who were not focusing on finding a man but on serving others, and while they did this, God couldn't help but send them His best.

First let's deal with Rebecca. Turn your Bible to Genesis 24: 4–26 and focus on verses fourteen through sixteen. Genesis 24:4–26 says,

> But thou shalt go unto my country, and to my kindred, and take a wife unto my son Isaac. 5. And the servant said unto him, Peradventure the woman will not be willing to follow me unto this land: must I needs bring thy son again unto the land from whence thou camest? 6. And Abraham said unto him, Beware thou that thou bring not my son thither again. 7. The Lord God of heaven, which took me from my father's house, and from the land of my kindred, and which spake Unto me, and that sware unto me, saying, Unto thy seed will I give this land; he shall send his angel before thee, and thou shalt take a wife unto my son from thence. 8. And if the woman will not be willing to follow thee, then thou shalt be clear from this my oath: only bring not my son thither again. 9. And the servant put his hand under the thigh of Abraham his master, and sware to

him concerning that matter. 10. And the servant took ten camels of the camels of his master, and departed; for all the goods of his master were in his hand: and he arose, and went to Mesopotamia, unto the city of Nahor. 11. And he made his camels to kneel down without the city by a well of water at the time of the evening, even the time that women go out to draw water. 12. *And he said O Lord God of my master Abraham, I pray thee, send me good speed this day, and shew kindness unto my master Abraham.* 13. Behold, I stand here by the well of water; and the daughters of the men of the city come out to draw water: 14. *And let it come to pass, that the damsel to whom I shall say, Let down thy pitcher, I pray thee, that I may drink; and she shall say, Drink, and I will give thy camels drink also: let the same be she that thou hast appointed for thy servant Isaac; and thereby shall I know that thou hast shewed kindness unto my master.* 15. *And it came to pass, before he had done speaking, that, behold, Rebekah came out, who was born to Bethuel, son of Milcah, the wife of Nahor, Abraham's brother, with her pitcher upon her shoulder.* 16. *And the damsel was very fair to look upon, a virgin, neither had any man known her: and she went down to the well, and filled her pitcher, and came up.* 17. *And the servant ran to meet her, and said, Let me, I pray thee, drink a little water of thy pitcher.* 18. *And she said, Drink, my lord: and she hasted, and let down her pitcher upon her hand, and gave him drink.* 19. *And when she had done giving him drink, she said, I will draw water for thy camels also, until they have done drinking.* 20. *And she hasted, and emptied her pitcher into the trough, and ran again unto the well to draw water, and drew for all his camels.* 21. And the man wondering at her

> held his peace, to wit whether the Lord had made his journey prosperous or not. 22. And it came to pass, as the camels had done drinking, that the man took a golden earring of half a shekel weight, and two bracelets for her hands of ten shekels weight of gold; 23. And said, Whose daughter art thou? tell me, I pray thee: is there room in thy father's house for us to lodge in? 24. And she said unto him, I am the daughter of Bethuel the son of Milcah, which she bare unto Nahor. 25. She said moreover unto him, We have both straw and provender enough, and room to lodge in. 26. And the man bowed down his head, and worshipped the Lord.
>
> Genesis 24:4–26 (emphasis added)

Abraham told his servant Eleazar to go find Isaac, Abraham's son a wife. Eleazar wanted to make sure that the woman he chose was God's choice, so he asked God to make sure *the woman loved to serve.* Verses twelve through fourteen prove this in saying,

> And he said O Lord God of my master Abraham, I pray thee, send me good speed this day, and shew kindness unto my master Abraham. 13. Behold, I stand here by the well of water; and the daughters of the men of the city come out to draw water: 14. And let it come to pass, that the damsel to whom I shall say, Let down thy pitcher, I pray thee, that I may drink; and she shall say, Drink, and I will give thy camels drink also: let the same be she that thou hast appointed for thy servant Isaac; and thereby shall I know that thou hast shewed kindness unto my master.

Now this day Rebecca was not going out looking for a man but instead was going out to serve. Now because she went out to serve, God placed in her spirit what to do to make sure she would catch the eye of the one seeking her. See while you have a mind to serve, God will place in you something to do that will catch the attention of your man. Here's *the key* again: *don't serve to be seen, serve to please God.*

Rebecca did a few things that prepared her for her man.

1. Even though she was going out to labor, she still looked good.

(Read verse sixteen)

Even though you are going to work, since you don't know when God will work the miracle, *always dress for success.* Never leave your house looking a mess. Wash your face, put lotion on your skin, wear something presentable, keep your nails looking nice, and please comb your hair.

2. She wasn't slow and lazy in her serving of others, but was diligent.

(Read verse eighteen) She hasted, meaning she did it quickly. Make sure you aren't one of those folk who serve and complain because you never know who's watching. Men are looking for a woman who doesn't complain or nag.

3. She went beyond the call of duty.

(Read verse nineteen) When you do things for others that are beyond the norm, not only do you move God, but you also move man. Set yourself apart from others. It was customary for women in those days to bring water to the man. But to serve his camel too, that's what I call setting yourself apart from the rest. Instead of just doing one thing, do extra to help others, and set yourself apart. When a man sees a woman who does not mind going beyond the call of duty, he sees a woman who doesn't mind working to have something in life. He says to himself, we can have something together because she's a go-getter.

4. Know whose daughter you are.

(Read verses twenty-three to twenty-four) Rebecca didn't know it, but Abraham told Eleazar to get Isaac a wife who was the daughter of Bethuel. So knowing who her father was connected her to her blessing. Woman of God, when you know that God is your Father you realize that this automatically connects you to your miracle. *God's son will always be looking for God's daughter.*

When you know also who your daddy is, you also know your daddy will hook you up when you do His will. God will send a man from another place or from out of nowhere. What I am trying to get you to see is your man may not come from your city, church, or even state, but when it is your time God will send the man from wherever He wants. Rebecca's man came from another state.

Psalm 84:11b promises you by saying, "no good thing will he withhold from them that walk uprightly."

The key to serving others is that most men are looking for a wife who will be a help, a support, and a lover. When men see women helping others, then they say to themselves, she will help me.

Let me give you one more example for you unbelievers out there to prove the point that these proven principles do work. I know you want to just catch a man with your looks, but when you just catch him with your looks, what if he meets someone else who looks just as good or better. But when you catch him with your looks and your heart to serve, then you set yourself apart from the crowd. Today's woman doesn't want to serve, but God's woman doesn't mind serving.

The next example of a woman who focused on serving was Ruth. Turn your Bible to Ruth 2:1–16, which reads:

> And Naomi had a kinsman of her husband's, a mighty man of wealth, of the family of Elimelech; and his name was Boaz. 2. And Ruth the Moabitess said unto Naomi, Let me now go to the field, and glean ears of corn after him in whose sight I shall find grace. And she said unto her, Go, my daughter. 3. And she went, and came, and gleaned in the field after the reapers: and her hap was to light on a part of the field belonging unto Boaz, who was of the kindred of Elimelech. 4. And, behold, Boaz came from Bethlehem, and said unto the reapers, The Lord be with you. And they answered him, The Lord bless thee. 5. Then said Boaz unto his servant that was set over the reapers, Whose damsel is this? 6. And the servant that was set over the reapers answered and said, It is the Moabitish damsel that came back with Naomi out of the country of Moab: 7. And she said I pray you, let me glean and gather after the reapers among the sheaves: so she came, and hath continued even from the morning until now, that she tarried a little in the house. 8. Then said Boaz unto Ruth,

Hearest thou not, my daughter? Go not to glean in another field, neither go from hence, but abide here fast by my maidens: 9. Let thine eyes be on the field that they do reap, and go thou after them: have I not charged the young men that they shall not touch thee? and when thou art athirst, go unto the vessels, and drink of that which the young men have drawn. 10. Then she fell on her face, and bowed herself to the ground, and said unto him, Why have I found grace in thine eyes, that thou shouldest take knowledge of me, seeing I am a stranger? 11. And Boaz answered and said unto her, it hath fully been shewed me, all that thou hast done unto thy mother in law since the death of thine husband: and how thou hast left thy father and thy mother, and the land of thy nativity, and art come unto a people which thou knewest not heretofore. 12. The Lord recompense thy work, and a full reward be given thee of the Lord God of Israel, under whose wings thou art come to trust. 13. Then she said, Let me find favour in thy sight, my lord; for that thou hast comforted me, and for that thou hast spoken friendly unto thine handmaid, though I be not like unto one of thine handmaidens. 14. And Boaz said unto her, At mealtime come thou hither, and eat of the bread, and dip thy morsel in the vinegar. And she sat beside the reapers: and he reached her parched corn, and she did eat, and was sufficed, and left. 15. And when she was risen up to glean, Boaz commanded his young men, saying, Let her glean even among the sheaves, and reproach her not: 16. And let fall also some of the handfuls of purpose for her, and leave them, that she may glean them, and rebuke her not.

To give you a little history, you are about to meet a woman named Ruth who was the daughter-in-law to a woman named Naomi. Naomi had a husband and two sons, of whom Ruth was married to one. Well, one day Naomi's husband died and left her a widow, then soon thereafter both her sons died now leaving Naomi and her two daughters-in-law broken. Orpah, one of the daughters-in-law decided to return back to her father's house, but Ruth decided to stay and take care of her mother-in-law.

1. Stop looking for a man
2. Focus all your attention on serving God and people
3. Even though you're going to serve, still look good
4. Don't serve and complain
5. Go beyond the call of duty (this will catch the eye)
6. Know whose daughter you are

1. Stop looking for a man.

Ruth, like many of us today, was hurt because of a past relationship. Ruth had just lost her man, and her heart was broken. Many times it's hard to be ready to look for Mr. Right when you are still hurt from the past. Our past hurt could have been death of loved one, a breakup, being cheated on, or being abused verbally and even physically. This broken heart makes it hard to trust again because a broken heart first must be healed, or whoever we get with will pay for the pain we had to endure. While Ruth was dealing with her pain, she took her focus off of her and focused on serving another. Here is step one again: take the focus off of yourself and stop looking for a man. In Ruth 1:16 Ruth says, "Intreat me not to leave thee, or to return from following after thee: for whither thou goest, I will go; and where thou lodgest, I will lodge: thy people shall be my people, and thy God my God."

Ruth was told by Naomi to go back to her father's house and seek a man because Naomi said she was too old to have another son to give to Ruth to marry. Ruth says, "No, I am not looking for a man; I want to seek after you and your God." You need to focus your attention on something else other than your hurt. The best one to turn to so you can get healed from your past is none other than the Lord. If you want a man, woman of God, just try this and truly turn your heart to God and keep your mind on Him. He promised in Isaiah 26:3, "Thou wilt keep him in perfect peace, whose mind is stayed on thee: because he trusteth in thee."

Now let's check out the other steps and see if there's success for another woman of God using these six steps.

2. Focus your attention on serving God and other people.

Again Ruth tells Naomi in verse sixteen for where you go I will go and where you lodge I will lodge. Then Ruth says,

> Let me now go to the field, and glean ears of corn after him in whose sight I shall find grace. And she said unto her, Go, my daughter. And she went, and came, and gleaned in the field after the reapers: and her hap was to light on a part of the field belonging unto Boaz, who was of the kindred of Elimelech.
>
> Ruth 2:2–3

So Ruth took her focus off herself, her hurt, and a man, and focused on serving Naomi. Woman of God, remember God keeps you single so you can do what pleases Him, and what pleases God is for you to love and care for another. Read verses four through eight which say:

> And, behold, Boaz came from Bethlehem, and said unto the reapers, The Lord be with you. And they answered him, The Lord bless thee. 5. Then said Boaz unto his servant that was set over the reapers, Whose damsel is this? 6. And the servant that was set over the reapers answered and said, It is the Moabitish damsel that came back with Naomi out of the country of Moab: 7. And she said, I pray you, let me glean and gather after the reapers among the sheaves: so she came, and hath continued even from the morning until now, that she tarried a little in the house. 8. Then said Boaz unto Ruth, Hearest thou not, my daughter? Go not to glean in another field, neither go from hence, but abide here fast by my maidens:
>
> Ruth 2:4–8

When Ruth decided to serve her mother-in-law and serve God, *the Lord strategically placed her in the place where her man could find her.* Verse three said she found herself gleaning in the field belonging to Boaz. God strategically placed her in the place where God could bless her because she decided to serve her mother-in-law. Woman of God, when you are serving others, God is gonna set you at the place where your man of God is gonna find you. *Are you ready for your miracle?*

The next step is step three:

3. Even though you go to serve, still look good.

Ruth, while on her way to the place of service, was warned by her mother-in-law, Naomi, and told by her to do three things when she left.

1. Wash yourself
2. Anoint yourself
3. Put some clothes on

First Ruth washed her face. Woman of God, keep yourself clean and smelling good. You never know when the Lord is going to send your man. I know that if you are in a place of serving, you won't always want to look your best. You may not get all made up, but make sure your face looks washed and fresh looking every time you leave that house.

The second thing Ruth did was anoint herself. Woman of God, keep your face and body lotion downed and looking fresh at all times. Now there are times when you may feel like you won't meet anybody today, but just when you say that, here he comes. Daughter, I want your face to be lotioned up, hands and arms (especially elbows) to look radiant, and if your legs and feet are showing, keep those legs shaved and lotioned and those toenails pedicured and lotioned. Whatever it takes please never come out looking ashy.

Anointing oil in Ruth's days also carried with it a fragrance. The oil had frankincense and myrrh in it that sent off a wonderful aroma in the room. You want to always smell good. You never know when you will have to give a brother a hug (Christian hug that is). You need to make sure that your underarms are always smelling good and that you always wear some perfume and deodorant. You don't always have to wear expensive perfume. Use your everyday perfume (but still smell good) for the introduction, and use your expensive perfume for the date. Always make sure you are clean and smell good.

The third principle was to put some clothes on. Woman of God, I know you may be going to places to serve others, or working for the Lord, or even on jobs that allow you to dress like you feel. First of all get that sentence out of your mouth that "I'm gonna dress how I feel." One thing a child of the Most High always has is joy. So your dress should be how you feel, and that is always joyous, even when life isn't happy. Happiness is dependent upon what happens, and everything in our lives doesn't happen the way we wished. Joy on the other hand is a characteristic of a saint and is not dependent on anything but your connection with the Holy Spirit. Make sure you always are dressed as a woman of God. You represent God, and our God is a God of dignity and honor. Remember how you dress will many times determine what you catch. It is like fishing, if I want to catch a scavenger like a catfish, most catfish will eat anything even trash. If I want to catch a crappie fish, I need to know that they are selective eaters. Same with men, woman of God, if you want scavengers remember they go after anything that looks like trash, but if you want a man that will respect you for who you are and not what you have, dress like a woman of God.

You never know when the Lord is going to send that man to the place where He has strategically placed you to be found. Be prepared for the miracle and always look good when you step out of your house. As you get up every morning, ask the Lord as you look through your closets and drawers, "Lord what would you have me to wear today that will glorify you." This is important because only God knows whom He is sending to you. And since He knows what this man likes, He will make sure to lead you to put on what will draw the man to you.

Naomi tells Ruth in Ruth 3:2b-3, "Behold, he winnoweth barley to night in the threshingfloor. Wash thyself therefore, and anoint thee, and put thy raiment upon thee, and get thee down to the floor: but make not thyself known unto the man, until he shall have done eating and drinking."

Naomi tells Ruth this night the man who the Lord has prepared for her is gonna be at an appointed place (the threshing floor) at an appointed time (at night), so she should get ready. Wash yourself, put on lotion and perfume, put on nice apparel, and serve like other times, but the key is to not say anything until the man has eaten and drunk. The last statement is key. If you want to get to a man, get to his stomach first by filling him with a good meal. Remember the way to a man's heart is through his stomach first. The point I want you to get is the same way Naomi told Ruth the time, Boaz would be at the expected place. God Himself told me to tell you, woman of God, that while you are serving others He will tell you the time and place when He will send to you your husband that He chose.

Remember 1 Corinthians 2:9, "But as it is written, Eye hath not seen, nor ear heard, neither have entered into the heart of man, the things which God hath prepared for them that love him."

There is someone God has prepared for you that no one else can have or ever know. The person God has for you is just for you. The key though is while you are serving others, 1

Corinthians 2:10 says, "But God hath revealed them unto us by his Spirit: for the Spirit searcheth all things, yea, the deep things of God." Now when God *knows* that you are *ready*, the Holy Spirit who dwells in you according to 1 Corinthians 3:16 will take you to the place and prepare you for the meeting of your life.

Are you ready? Some of you ask, pastor, when I meet a man, how do I know he is Mr. Right? First don't tell him you are a Christian at first, but let him talk and show his cards. Once he reveals who he truly is, then tell him you are a daughter of God.

Now for the *men* there are some biblical principles that God has given you, which if you follow you will meet the perfect woman for you. Fellow brothers, I know that Satan always is trying to get us to make that mistake of getting physical first. You have to fight this desire because once the physical relationship occurs, your soul becomes connected to that woman even if she is totally wrong for you. Read Genesis 34:2–3 where there was a man named Shechem, a Hivite, who desired Dinah the daughter of Jacob so much that he went and had sex with her. The key point is found in verses two and three where it says,

> And when Shechem the son of Hamor the Hivite, prince of the country, *saw her, he took her,* and *lay with her*, and defiled her. *And his soul clave unto Dinah* the daughter of Jacob, and he loved the damsel, and spake kindly unto the damsel.
>
> Genesis 34:2–3 (emphasis added)

He after being connected to her in sex became connected to

her in his soul which includes his mind, emotions, and will. You won't be able to think spiritually, have spiritual emotions, or make sound spiritual decisions when you become connected to a woman in relations before marriage. Also read 1 Corinthians 6:15–19 with focus on verses sixteen to seventeen to see the picture of you connecting with a woman that could cause you harm and a disconnection with the Lord. First Corinthians 6:15–19 reads,

> Know ye not that your bodies are the members of Christ? Shall I then take the members of Christ, and make them the members of a harlot [person involved in sexual sin]? God forbid. 16. What? Know ye not that *he which is joined to a harlot is one body*? For *two, saith he, shall be one flesh.* 17. But he that is joined unto the Lord is one spirit. 18. Flee fornication. Every sin that a man doeth is without the body; but he that *committeth fornication sinneth against his own body.* 19. What? Know ye not that *your body is the temple of the Holy Ghost which is in you*, which ye have of God, and ye are not your own?
>
> 1 Corinthians 6:15–19 (emphasis added)

1 Corinthians 7:32b tells us that, "He that is unmarried careth for the things that belong to the Lord, how he may please the Lord." Man of God, you are single now because God needs you to complete your assignment with Him first before your focus will change. First Corinthians 7:33 says, "But he that is married careth for the things that are of the world, how he may please his wife." Once you become married, you will not

be able to focus your attention on doing the Lord's work. Once you fulfill your assignment God says in Psalm 84:11c, "No good thing will the Lord withhold from them that walk uprightly." Then Psalm 62:5 tells us, "My soul, wait thou only upon God; for my expectation is from him." The thing I am expecting or looking for, the wife that I will have comes from God.

Now brother I don't want you to just have a woman, but a wife. *Every woman is not a wife.* A wife has something special about her that completes you. Adam was put to sleep by God, and a rib was taken from him and used to make a woman. Adam, when receiving his wife from God, said "this is now bone of my bones, and flesh of my flesh: she shall be called Woman" (Genesis 2:23). Adam recognized that she came out of him and without her he was incomplete. The wife you choose ought to add to you and make you feel complete with her. Your wife will come to you from the Lord.

Proverbs 19:14b says, "A prudent wife is from the Lord." God will bring to you a prudent woman. The word *prudent* in the Greek means:

- to be intelligent
- able to be instructed
- skillful
- has good success
- able to teach
- has gift of understanding and wisdom
- guides wittingly

So the woman God will send you will have all these attributes, and when you find this woman then Proverbs 18:22 comes into play which says, "Whoso findeth a wife findeth a good thing, and obtaineth favour of the Lord." In other words when you find her not only will she be a good one, but together the favor and blessings of God will overtake you because you are walking with the gift of God.

The question you are asking me is, pastor, how do I find such a woman. Well, first of all find her serving the Lord. If you want a woman who will love you, first find her loving the Lord. Look for her at places where she is serving others. (Places like the church, hospitals, convalescent homes, group homes, etc). *Remember if she has a heart to love and serve a stranger, she will definitely have the heart and love to serve you.* Make sure she has a heart for people, which means she has a lot of love to give. It also means she's not selfish, not self-centered, not greedy, and not high minded. It does mean she's giving, loving, caring, and puts others' needs before hers. That's a woman you need. Out of all good marriages, the wives God chooses are always found serving.

Example of great wives found serving:

1. Isaac finds Rebecca serving (Genesis 24:16–20)
2. Moses finds Zipphora taking care of her father's business (Exodus 2:16, 21)
3. Boaz finds Ruth serving her mother in law (Ruth 2:10, 11–13)

Men of God, remember that God has said through the Apostle Paul not to be unequally yoked together with unbelievers. If she is not saved, don't tie the knot. Before you say I do, here are some suggestions on picking a wife.

1. Pray and ask the Holy Spirit for direction- Be specific in your desires.
2. Look for a woman who loves God and His people
3. When you find a woman and take her on a date, allow her to talk and she will tell you all about herself. Ask about her dreams, goals, desires, and see if she thinks outside the box.
4. If the relationship is serious, visit her mother and watch how she operates. In most cases the daughter is a clone of her mother.
5. Observe her strengths and weaknesses and see if her strengths are your weaknesses, and your strengths are her weaknesses. If this is the case, you have a good match.
6. Ask your heavenly Father to show the true her to you.

I'm a Widow (Is It Over?)

Woman or man of God whose husband or wife has moved on to glory, the fact that you are reading this book means you are ready to move forward. Very few people can understand your pain, your loneliness, and your late-night tears. When you really love someone and they are no longer here, it feels like a part of you has been stripped or dissected off of you. This makes sense because the Word of God said that the husband shall be joined to the wife and the two shall be one flesh. This means you are one, and the separation means a part of you was taken away.

First of all remember that if God allowed it to happen, there is something He has in store just for you. You have to know that because the Lord called your honey home doesn't mean that your life is over. When God made you, He attached purpose and plans to your life, and many times He knows that your married state hindered the fulfillment of your purpose. So now that you are able to do so, focus on the Lord, and He will direct you to what He wants to do through you. I know you're saying, pastor, I can't go on without my honey, but you don't have time to just wait. Time is ticking, and your own days are numbered. John 9:4 says, "I must work the works of him that sent me, while it is day: the night cometh, when no man can work."

How Do I Cope with the Loss?

The word cope means finding a place of peace in an adverse situation. Well you are asking, how do you cope with the loss. I have had to watch my mother learn how to cope with the loss of my father, and one thing I saw her do was find refuge in the arms of the Lord. Child of God, the Lord will allow pain to come to drive you closer to Him, and you need to be like Job in Job 13:15 and tell the devil, "Though he slay me yet will I trust him." David gave us some hope in Psalms 34:17–19 by saying,

> The righteous cry, and the Lord heareth, and delivereth them out of all their troubles. 18. The Lord is nigh unto them that are of a broken heart; and saveth such as be of a contrite spirit. 19. Many are the afflictions of the righteous: but the Lord delivereth him out of them all.

David tells us in the Scripture that when you are crying and wondering what you are going to do, God hears your cry. David says, I make you a promise that if you cry the Lord will deliver you out of all your troubles. Child of God, in those late night hours when you can't sleep, I dare you to cry out to God and watch Him see you through. David says in verse eighteen that the Lord is close to those whose heart is broken. If you want to know who God spends time with, find a brokenhearted person. Have you ever been brokenhearted and wondered how you came through? I want you to know that even in your brokenness, the Lord was there and kept you from going insane. Finally in verse nineteen, David tells us that as a child of God, it is guaranteed that we will have many afflictions, but God guarantees us that He will deliver us out of all of them. You should be shouting right now because even though you go through a storm, don't forget that your storm is nothing but an opportunity for the Lord to speak peace over it. Also in Psalms 42:1–5 David tells us,

> As the hart panteth after the water brooks, so panteth my soul after thee, O God. 2. My soul thirsteth for God, for the living God: when shall I come and appear before God? 3. My tears have been my meat day and night, while they continually say unto me, Where is thy God? 4. When I remember these things, I pour out my soul in me: for I had gone with the multitude, I went with them to the house of God, with the voice of joy and praise, with a multitude that kept holyday. 5. Why art thou cast down, O my soul? and why art thou disquieted in me? Hope thou in God: for I shall yet praise him for the help of his countenance.

David says in verses one through three he could not eat, sleep, or even want to do anything but cry. His tears were so heavy that he cried himself to sleep every night. Verse four says that David went to the house of God with the praisegivers to the Church, and they shouted; *but David wondered why he was there.*

Then verse five says something inside of him asked "why are you worried and fretting?" He hoped in God, for even in his affliction he would yet praise God's name. You have to have the attitude that no matter what comes your way that you will be determined to walk with Jesus all the way. He wants you to remember what He told his disciples in Mark 4:40, "Why are ye so fearful? How is it that ye have no faith?"

God told you before that He was going to take you to another level in Him, but just like the disciples He never told you about the storm you would face on the way. In the latter part of verse forty Jesus asks the disciples where their faith is. In other words, didn't I tell you I would see you through to the other side? God did not always promise the road would be easy, but He promised never to leave you alone.

The other thing I saw my mother do was *find her purpose in her loss*. She asked the Lord, what would He have her do. You don't have time to sit in that pity party. Get yourself up and pull it together, God has a job for you to do. Your life is not finished; just a chapter has ended, but that just means a new chapter is beginning. Find your purpose or the plan that God has for you. Teaching, helping those in need, or ministering to the Lord in worship are great purposes. There was a widow in Luke 2:36 named Anna who was married for seven years at a young age and lost her husband. The Bible says for fourscore and four years (eighty-four years) she stayed in the temple and ministered to God. The Bible called her a prophetess. In other words she did not sit along the wayside and throw a pity party. She went in and got so close to the

Lord that the Lord spoke prophetic words to her to give to the people. Read about Naomi in Ruth 1:20, which says, "And she said unto them, Call me not Naomi, call me Mara [meaning bitterness]: for the almighty hath dealt very bitterly with me." Naomi was bitter because her husband died but she realized her purpose was to be able to prepare her widowed daughter in law for her miracle. By her doing this, God blessed Naomi as it says in Ruth 4:14: "And the women said unto Naomi, Blessed be the Lord, which hath not left thee this day without a kinsman [blessing in the midst of your pain], that his name may be famous in Israel."

The third thing my mother did to move on after my father was to know in her heart that while he was here she did all she could to satisfy him within her ability. This made her feel like she did her part for the season the Lord lent him to her. God wants your loved ones to have peace with Him in glory, and if you really love them you ought to want the same for them.

Do I Still Have It?

Have you asked yourself the question, "Do I still have it?" Once someone goes through years of pouring out themselves into their spouse emotionally, physically, and mentally they sometime ask the question "Do I have any more of myself left to give?" You have given out a whole lot and in some cases have not received even half as much in return from that loved one. Starting over again can be a frightening thought, but my sister and brother, I want to encourage you that it's possible that God has someone out there who He has prepared for you who wants to pour out and give of them for you. Do you still have it? Yes, you do! You got it going on. I don't care if you are not what you would like to be (in size, age, or state of mind), but the truth of the matter is your confidence will dictate your success.

I want you to say this to yourself right now: "*I still got it goin' on!*"

I don't know if you knew this or not but there are biblical examples of people that wondered if they still had it. There are a few I'd like to share with you to encourage you to get out there and take life by the horns and ride it. Pick yourself up, get your mind right, and tell yourself that the best is yet to come. Who told you that you can't experience more happiness in your life? Who told you that because your loved one has moved residences that God wants you to just be alone and not experience being loved again by someone else He sends you? Look at Genesis 38:6–26 which says,

> And Judah took a wife for Er his firstborn, whose name was Tamar. 7. And Er, Judah's firstborn, was wicked in the sight of the Lord; and the Lord slew him. 8. And Judah said unto Onan, Go in unto thy brother's wife, and marry her, and raise up seed to thy brother. 9. And Onan knew that the seed should not be his; and it came to pass, when he went in unto his brother's wife, that he spilled it on the ground, lest that he should give seed to his brother. 10. And the thing which he did displeased the Lord: wherefore he slew him also. 11. Then said Judah to Tamar his daughter in law, Remain a widow at thy father's house, *till Shelah my son be grown*: for he said, Lest

peradventure he die also, as his brethren did. And Tamar went and dwelt in her father's house. 12. And in process of time the daughter of Shuah Judah's wife died; and Judah was comforted, and went up unto his sheepshearers to Timnath, he and his friend Hirah the Adullamite. 13. And it was told Tamar, saying, Behold thy father in law goeth up to Timnath to shear his sheep. 14. And she put her widow's garments off from her, and covered her with a vail, and wrapped herself, and sat in an open place, which is by the way to Timnath; for she saw that Shelah was grown, and she was not given unto him to wife. 15. When Judah saw her, he thought her to be an harlot; because she had covered her face. 16. And he turned unto her by the way, and said, Go to, I pray thee, let me come in unto thee; (for he knew not that she was his daughter in law.) And she said, What wilt thou give me, that thou mayest come in unto me? 17. And he said, I will send thee a kid from the Flock. And she said, Wilt thou give me a pledge, till thou send it? 18. And he said, *What pledge shall I give thee*? And she said, Thy signet, and thy Bracelets, and thy staff that is in thine hand. And he gave it her, and came in unto her, and she conceived by him. 19. And she arose, and went away, and laid by her vail from her, and put on the garments of her widowhood. 20. And Judah sent the kid by the hand of his friend the Adullamite, to receive his pledge from the woman's hand: but he found her not. 21. Then he asked the men of that place, saying, *Where is the harlot*, that was openly by the way side? And they said, There was no harlot in this place. 22. And he returned to Judah, and said, I cannot find her; and also the men of the place said,

> that there was no harlot in this place. 23. And Judah said, Let her take it to her, lest we be shamed: behold, I sent this kid, and thou hast not found her. 24. And it came to pass about three months after, that it was told Judah, saying, Tamar thy daughter in law hath played the harlot; and also, behold, she is with child by whoredom. And Judah said, Bring her forth, and let her be burnt. 25. When she was brought forth, she sent to her father in law, saying, By the man, whose these are, am I with child: and she said, Discern, I pray thee, whose are these, the signet, and bracelets, and staff. 26. And Judah acknowledged them, and said, She hath been more righteous than I; because that I gave her not to Shelah my son. And he knew her again no more.
>
> Genesis 38:6–26 (emphasis added)

In this passage of Scripture we find Tamar, a woman who's hurt and wondering what's left for her, after God has allowed her to go through tribulation after tribulation. First of all her husband, Er, dies and leaves her with no child. In those days a Jewish woman's whole fulfillment in life was to have a male child to carry on the name of her husband. Anyone who didn't was considered by society as being cursed by God. Her husband dies, and her father-in-law feels sorry for her and gives her his next son, Onan, in verse nine. Onan doesn't want to have a child with her knowing this was his brother's wife so he spills his semen on the ground, and God is angered by this and kills him. Now Tamar has lost two husbands and still has no child. She's feeling all dried up. Can't you see her, look at her? She's sitting in a room all alone with her head buried in her hands with tears in her eyes asking herself "can I go on?" What tops it off is that after all of this her father-in-law tells her to back to her father's house and wait until his youngest son grows up, and then they'll see what happens.

I don't know what you really want in life, but Tamar wanted a child. You may be missing love, peace, fulfillment, someone who just loves, companionship, but whatever it is don't do what Tamar did, but have the same mindset that she has. Her mindset was "I'm going to fight for what is rightfully mine," so Tamar goes back home. Can you see her? Not only has life dealt her a bad deal, but now she has to go back home and move back in with her parents. Reading this book you may be at the point where you have lost your loved one, and financially or emotionally you cannot handle being alone. You had to go back home just like Tamar and wonder to yourself, "do I have anything left?"

Remember the thing in Tamar's life that was most important for her to receive to feel like her life was fulfilled, she still has never received. Her need was to have a child, but the question is "what's your need?" What's that one thing you've never received, even in your marriage that you know you deserved? Was it:

1. Happiness
2. Feeling truly loved
3. Financial stability
4. Accomplishing your dream
5. Feeling appreciated

6. Traveling outside of the state line or (for some of us) county line
7. Peace
8. __________(you fill in)

Well here's what I want you to do. First, don't do what Tamar does in verses fourteen through twenty-four, but I do want you to have the same drive Tamar has. She walks in four very strong and attractive ways:

1. I'm not all dried up
2. If I'm still here, there's still hope
3. I won't let life take me; I'm taking life
4. I deserve to get what I want!

It's not over, and today I want you to walk in the mindset of Tamar and that is for you even as a man or woman. You deserve what you want and know that God has promised you in Psalm 84:11b, "No good thing will the Lord withhold from them that walk uprightly." God will not hold back from you what you deserve.

Psalm 34:10b says, "They that seek the Lord shall not want any good thing." The Lord tells you that if you seek Him you shall not want any good thing. In other words every desire you have you will receive if you put the Lord first.

Should I Just Let it Go?

Did you know that the average widow or divorcee says to themselves, there's no reason for me to live anymore? Six out of ten widows fall into deep states of depression and feel destitute after the loss of their loved one. I'm glad today that you who are reading this book have declared to yourself, "I shall not die but live." I'm glad I'm not talking to a quitter but an achiever. I'm glad that you will not lie down and lose your strength to keep marching on, but instead you feel like being the poster child for those who say "I'm a survivor."

First Timothy 5:5 tells us what to do; it says "Now he or she that is a widow indeed, and desolate, *trusteth in God*, and continueth in supplications and prayers night and day" (emphasis added). Now the verse continues, but I want you to just focus on that part that is italicized. Do you trust God? Do you believe, and I mean believe that if God allowed something to happen to you, somehow it is going to work for your good? Romans 8:28 says, "And we know that all things work together for good to them that love God, to them who are the called according to his purpose."

So you ask, pastor, are you saying that God wanted this to happen. Was the home going of my wife or husband planned by God? I am saying that God lent them to us for a season. They belong to Him first, and Psalm 116:15 says, "Precious in the sight of the Lord is the death of his saints." God did not want them to suffer anymore or be down here anymore for whatever purpose. For some reason and purpose you are at the right place and the right season of your life to move to the next level in faith toward God. To prove this to you, read the second part of 1 Timothy 5:5 where it says, *that the widow continues* (didn't stop even when Satan told you to just give up) *in supplications* (written petitions to God for your desire, with your hand laid on the paper believing God to do it) *and prayers night and day.*

God has caused this to happen to draw you closer to him. Don't let go! Don't give up! Don't say it's over! No it's not; it's just that chapter in your life God finished, but now He's already writing a new chapter. I hope you don't miss it. Don't forget *the Lord* is the Author and Finisher of our faith.

Do I Want to Do It All Over Again?

I know some of you are saying, pastor, I have spent the majority of my life catering to my spouse. I am now at a point where I can live for me. Then some of us are saying I went through hell in that marriage. I've been hurt, mentally (and for some) physically abused, mistreated, unappreciated, and underpaid. I don't want to have to go through that all over again. Then we have those of us who are saying I'm not sure I want to go through the process of building from start again. Pastor, it's like starting a race from the beginning all over again.

My response to all three types of responses is the same. "You don't know what's behind door number three." You may be saying pastor, what are you talking about? I'm glad you asked. *Door number one is your past* (for some it contains good days and for some bad days), but the key is it's closed now and the only one who can open it is you. The Apostle Paul told us in Philippians 3:13b: "Forgetting those things which are behind, and reaching forth unto those things which are before."

In other words it's okay to hold on to good memories, but let go of the bad and the past. *Better days are up ahead*! Only you know your present state of mind and heart. You may try to fool us by saying, "I'm doing fine." The truth from all mankind is that *everyone wants to* be loved. Your present is just what it says, your present and where you *stand right now.* This means this is the place where you can decide to either move forward with you only or with you and God walking hand in hand to get your gift behind door number three. You serve a God of progression, and He will not sit with you in a place of apathy or complacency.

So what's behind door number three, you ask. Well I don't know. The only way we'll find out is if you get up from where you are and stop fearing about the unknown and trust that if the Lord created the door, He also created the gift behind it. Remember this saying because it will help you cope with fearing people hurting you. Even your hurtful times taught you lessons that helped you. Here is a saying that helps: "the creature can never do more than what the Creator let's them do." In other words, if God allows it, somehow it's working for your good.

The key in all of this is that I want you to have your confidence in the Lord. In Philippians 4:11b Paul says, "For I have learned in whatsoever state I am [whatever God has put me in] therewith to be content." Paul says if God put him at this juncture of his life, he trusts that God knows what's best for him. Be content, hold your head up, and put a smile on your face, because you belong to God.

Controlling the Beast That's Used to Being Fed

The beast is your sex drive that married life awakened and fed. Now the Lord has called your loved one home, and you are suppose to just make it go to sleep. Some think a widow should be like the prophetess Anna in Luke 2:36–37, which describes Anna after her husband died. She stayed in the temple praying and fasting and never being with someone again. Not all of us are that strong. When you are use to having sex on a normal basis and now suddenly it ends, you may be missing your spouse; but some of us are saying, I wish someone would tell my body to sleep and hibernate. Now the test begins. For some the test will be easy because either you are truly rooted and grounded in the Lord, or your spouse made sexual intercourse feel like a boring movie (always put you to sleep) or a splinter in your finger (irritating and in most cases painful).

I'm not worried about you all, but I am worried about the one who is going through the test of the beast wanting to feed because it's used to being fed. You have it harder than most people, and if you can crucify your flesh God will bless you. To control the beast (the sexual drive) you have to:

1. Shackle Him
2. Cage Him
3. Tame Him

The best way to shackle the sexual desire is to know what places the beast shows up. Every natural beast has a place and time where they like to feed. Wherever your beast tries to feed is the place where you have to stay away from. The sexual drive is nothing more than your flesh, and your flesh can't live in power unless it is fed. Galatians 5:17 says, "For the flesh lusteth against the Spirit, and the Spirit against the flesh: and these are contrary the one to the other: so that ye cannot do the things that ye would."

You would obey the Word of God, but when your flesh is trying to feed, you have to keep him from the place where it is fed. Don't get caught with a man in a secluded place, and if you are a man, don't get caught with a woman in a precarious situation. Weaken the beast with Scriptures like:

1. Galatians 5:19–21

> Now the works of the flesh are manifest, which are these; *Adultery, fornication*, uncleanness, lasciviousness, 20. Idolatry, witchcraft, hatred, variance, emulations, wrath, strife, seditions, heresies, 21. Envyings, murders, drunkenness, revellings, and such like: of the which I tell you before, as I have also told you in time past, *that they which do such things shall not inherit the kingdom of God.*
>
> (emphasis added)

2. Ephesians 5:5

> "For this ye know, *that no whoremonger*, nor unclean person, nor covetous man, who is an idolater, *hath any inheritance in the kingdom of Christ and of God*"
>
> (emphasis added)

3. 1 Corinthians 6:16–20

> What? know ye not that *he which is joined to an harlot is one body*? for *two, saith he, shall be one flesh*. 17. But he that is joined unto the Lord is one spirit. 18. *Flee fornication*. Every sin that a man doeth is without the body; but *he that committeth fornication sinneth against his own body*. 19. What? know ye not that *your*

> *body is the temple of the Holy Ghost which is in you,* which ye have of God, and ye are not your own? 20. *For ye are bought with a price*: therefore *glorify God in your body, and in your spirit, which are God's.*"
>
> (emphasis added)

4. Mark 7:21–23

> "For from within, *out of the heart of men*, *proceed* evil thoughts, *adulteries, fornications*, murders, 22. Thefts, covetousness, wickedness, deceit, lasciviousness, an evil eye, blasphemy, pride, foolishness: 23. *All these evil things come from within, and defile the man.*"

The second way to solve the problem is to cage the beast (sexual drive). Well you can't cage certain beasts until you either shoot them or weaken them. The same with the sex demon, you can't cage it until you first weaken it. To cage a beast, you have to shoot it with a tranquilizer gun or lure it into a place by making it think it is going one place and taking into a place of confinement.

You need to weaken the beast with the Word of God, which is your spiritual tranquilizer gun, and then put it into its cage away from other wild beasts like it. Keep yourself in Bible study and a worship service and get involved in the ministry and keep busy working for the Lord. Get yourself in a place where you can keep your mind on the Lord because Isaiah 26:3 tells us that, "Thou wilt keep him in perfect peace, whose mind is stayed on thee: because he trusteth in thee." God will keep you in peace (a place of not being wild) if you keep your mind on Him.

Then finally the third way to address sexuality is to tame

the beast (sexual drive). The best way to tame a beast is to teach it another way to live and keep its mind from the wild nature. You have to remember that the old nature will always try to attack your mind because if Satan can get you to think about it, he can get you to do it. You need to train your mind to stop thinking about sex. A great Scripture that tells us how to tame our mind is 2 Corinthians 10:4–5 which says,

> For the weapons of our warfare are not carnal, but mighty through God [spiritual weapons like: prayer, fasting, and in your Word] to the pulling down of strong holds; Casting down imaginations, and every high thing that exalteth itself against the knowledge of God, and bringing into captivity every thought to the obedience of Christ.

Verse five says again to tame him, then cage your thoughts. It says bring into captivity every thought to the obedience of Christ. In other words to tame your mind, stop letting bad thoughts even get into your mind. When you feel that thought trying to rise up in your mind, rehearse 2 Corinthians 10:4–5. Tell the devil, "devil, I rebuke any wicked thought from coming into my mind." Cast down imaginations or subtle messages or visions that try to come into your mind. You have to tame the beast by renewing your mind. Colossians 3:5,6,10 tells us,

> Mortify [crush, put down, put to shame] therefore your members which are upon the earth; *fornication*, uncleanness, *inordinate affection*, evil concupiscence, and *covetousness*, *which is idolatry*: 6. For all these

> things' sake the wrath of God cometh on the children of disobedience: 10. And have put on the new man, which is renewed in knowledge after the image of him that created him:
>
> Colossians 3:5–6, 10 (emphasis added)

You have to know that you have to change the way you see yourself. Renew your knowledge to see yourself as an exact image of God in the human form. Would God let the sex demon have rule over Him? Why then are you?

Biography of Dr. Allen S. Turner

Dr. Allen S. Turner is the pastor of St. Matthew's Baptist Church in Livermore, California, with a congregation of over 800 and growing. He also is the founder and president of God's Love Outreach Ministries, which oversees the chaplain ministry of the fifth largest jail in the country in Alameda County California.

Pastor Turner is a native Californian. Upon graduation from California High School in San Ramon, California, he attended Texas Christian University in Fort Worth, Texas. He later received his teaching credentials and a Doctorate of Divinity in Biblical Studies from the Sacramento Theological Seminary and Bible College in 2004.

Pastor Turner is very busy doing God's work:

- **Teaching:** He teaches degreed education programs to church members and the community at large through the Sacramento Theological Seminary and Bible College.

- **Founding ministries:** A progressive leader, Pastor Turner continues the legacy started by his late father to spread the Gospel beyond the walls of St. Matthew's to the community, the state, and throughout the world. He founded God's Love Outreach Ministries. As a result many new ministries are operating under GLOM.
- **Youth Ministry Outreach:** Realizing today's youth are "at risk" spiritually and morally, Pastor Turner is devoted to providing spiritual outlets in which our children can learn and grow.
- **Youth Tutoring Program:** The tutoring program has been instrumental in raising grade point averages from 2.0 and lower to a minimum of 3.0.
- **God's Love Christian Academy:** An accredited curriculum for Pre-Kindergarten through fourth grade.
- **Youth Christian Club:** Supervised Christian youth can fellowship together with the community on the weekend to provide their own entertainment through talent shows, displaying their talents in singing, gospel rap, traditional gospel, praise dancing, and performing arts.
- **Sponsored Youth conferences:** The conferences are designed to enrich and empower our youth to become future leaders.

Pastor Turner provides spiritual consulting and counseling to at-risk and tragedy stricken youth at the Livermore High School.

Sponsoring youth career development workshops and

activities that provide avenues for encouraging youth at an early age to begin thinking about college.

Other Outreach Ministries

Chaplain services for the Alameda County Prison Ministry. This ministry provides an opportunity to minister to over 6,000 souls daily for Santa Rita Jail and Glenn Dyer Jail.

God's Love Transitional Home for Families. The home initially slotted to be a haven for battered, abused and previously incarcerated women, has been expanded to include temporary housing for families in need.

Pastor Turner is on the Human Services Commission for the City of Livermore.

He has authored three books: *The Servant's Hands—A Deacon's Handbook*, *Hear the Sound of God's Voice*, and now *Saved Singles Surviving a Seductive Society*.

Pastor Turner continues to develop community relationships with the city of Livermore, the counties of Contra Costa, Alameda and San Joaquin, and the State of California. With over hundreds of churches in the Alameda County, Governor Schwarzenegger chose Pastor Turner to participate in the Governor's Luncheon.

Pastor Turner married his childhood love, Minister Yolanda Turner. They have four children: Lamar De'Andre; Adojinah; and twin girls, Alaisha and Ashley.

Pastor Turner has a genuine love for his sheep and a passionate desire to ensure that all who are entrusted in his care will be welcomed in heaven when God deems to call them home.

Endnotes

1. Webster's II New Riverside University Dictionary
2. Webster's II New Riverside University Dictionary